¡Mira!

Anneli McLachlan

2

www.heinemann.co.uk
✓ Free online support
✓ Useful weblinks
✓ 24 hour online ordering

01865 888080

Heinemann is an imprint of Pearson Education Limited, a company incorporated in England and Wales, having its registered office at Edinburgh Gate, Harlow, Essex, CM20 2JE. Registered company number: 872828

www.heinemann.co.uk

Heinemann is the registered trademark of Pearson Education Limited

Text © Harcourt Education Limited, 2007

First published 2007

12 11 10 09
10 9 8 7 6 5 4

British Library Cataloguing in Publication Data is available from the British Library on request.

ISBN 978 0 435391 94 2

Edited by Naomi Laredo
Managing Editor: Iñaki Alegre
Designed by Ken Vail Graphic Design, Cambridge
Typeset by Ken Vail Graphic Design, Cambridge
Original illustrations © Harcourt Education Limited 2007

Illustrated by Graham-Cameron Illustration (David Benham),Clive Goodyer, Sylvie Poggio Artists Agency (Tim Davies, Mark Ruffle, Rory Walker), Ken Laidlaw, Young Digital Poland.

Picture research by Christine Martin & Susi Paz

Cover photo © Getty Images

Printed in China (EPC/04)

Acknowledgements
Harcourt and the author would like to thank Liliana Acosta Uribe, Iñaki Alegre, Clive Bell, Gillian Eades, Alex Harvey, Christopher Lillington and Ana Machado. They would also like to thank Colegio Betulia (Badalona), Elena Roig, Lidia Verges, Albert Campamany, Martí Riverola, Clara Fabregat, José María Bazán of Nordqvist Productions and all those involved with the recordings for their invaluable help in the development and trialling of this course.

The author and publisher would like to thank the following individuals and organisations for permission to reproduce photographs:

Alami pp**27** (football), **46** (taking photos), **55** (turtle), **81** (girl in uniform), **98** (jewellery shop – Andrew Holt), **98** (music shop – Brand X Pictures), **182** (Mar del Plata – David R Frazier Photolibrary Inc), **96** & **102** (Barcelona & Sagrada Familia – Medioimages), **57** & **96** (Dalí & Picasso – Popperfoto), **98** (shoe shop – Snappdragon), **93** (Poncho – World Pictures); Corbis pp**11** (Enrique Iglesias, Alejandro Sanz & Shakira), **43** (musicians in Cuba), **46** (listening to music), **84** (Chapelco), **96** (Amusement Park), **98** (baker's, supermarket), **108** (Emperor Trajano, Isabel la Católica, King Juan Carlos I); Dreamstime. com pp**86** & **122** (Dolores & Cintia – Jaimie Duplas), **84** (Calafate – Mercedes Soledad Manrique), **60** (chicken wings – Rohit Seth), **46** (sunbathing – Roman Milert); Getty Images pp**24** (table football), **14** (Margaret – PhotoDisc), **33** (Tatiana – PhotoDisc), **43** (Eiffel Tower – PhotoDisc), **44** (plane – PhotoDisc), **75** (Alcázar de Toledo – PhotoDisc); iStockPhoto.com pp**24** (disco), **46** (flamenco, volleyball), **123** (Manchester – Jonathan Klemenz), **47** (Rico – Leah-Anne Thompson), **43** (Dominican Republic – Oksana Struk); Photos.com pp.**24** (bowling alley), **60** (cereal), **82** (brown boots); RCA pp**11** (Christina Aguilera); Rex Features pp**66** (Beckham – Masatoshi Okauchi); Spanish Embassy pp**108** (Abd al Rahman III), **111** (Gaudí); StockDisc pp**46** (mobile). All other photos were provided by Jules Selmes, Tudor Photography, Carlos Reyez-Manzo, Gareth Boden and Harcourt Education Limited.

Every effort has been made to contact copyright holders of material reproduced in this book. Any omissions will be rectified in subsequent printings if notice is given to the publishers.

Tel: 01865 888088 www.heinemann.co.uk

Contenidos

¡Buen trabajo!
¡Bien hecho!
¡Buena idea!
¡Lo has hecho muy bien!
¡Qué interesante!
¡Genial!
¡Excelente!
¡Estupendo!
¡Has sacado un 10!
¡Está perfecto!

Good work!
Well done!
Good idea!
You did that really well!
How interesting!
Great!
Excellent!
Fantastic!
You got 10/10!
Perfect!

¡Atención!
Cuidado con los acentos.
Cuidado con las concordancias.
Cuidado con tu ortografía.
¿Cómo se puede mejorar?
¿Puedes poner un ejemplo?
¿Voluntarios?

Careful!
Careful with the accents.
Careful with the agreements.
Careful with your spelling.
How can it be improved?
Can you give an example?
Who can help?

Tienes que mejorar.
Tienes que hacerlo otra vez.
Tienes que repetir.
Tienes que mejorar tu ortografía.
Escribe cinco veces: ...

You need to improve.
You need to do this again.
You need to repeat this.
You need to improve your spelling.
Write ... five times.

La gente

1

1 Presentaciones

- Talking about activities
- Expressing opinions using **me gusta**.

escuchar 1 Escucha a Fernanda Famosa y escribe la letra correcta. (1–8)
Listen to Fernanda Famosa and write down the correct letter.

Ejemplo: **1** d

¿Qué haces en tu tiempo libre?

a
Chateo por internet.

b
Mando mensajes.

c
Bailo.

d
Escucho música.

e
Juego con el ordenador.

f
Voy de compras.

g
Salgo con mis amigos.

h
Hago deporte.

Gramática

Spanish verb endings change to show who the verb refers to.

¿Escuch**as** música? *Do **you** listen to music?*
Escuch**o** música. *I listen to music.*

Some verbs are irregular. Try to remember these:

	hacer *(to do)*	salir *(to go out)*	ir *(to go)*
(yo) *(I)*	hago	salgo	voy
(tú) *(you)*	haces	sales	vas

Para saber más   **página 129**

hablar 2 Con tu compañero/a, empareja las preguntas con las respuestas del ejercicio 1.
With your partner, match up the questions with the answers from exercise 1.

- ¿Sales con amigos?
- Salgo con mis amigos.

1 ¿Sales con amigos?   **5** ¿Chateas por internet?
2 ¿Mandas mensajes?   **6** ¿Juegas con el ordenador?
3 ¿Escuchas música?   **7** ¿Vas de compras?
4 ¿Bailas?   **8** ¿Haces deporte?

escribir 3 Escribe un texto sobre ti. *Write a text about yourself.*

Ejemplo: En mi tiempo libre mando mensajes y voy de compras.
También salgo con mis amigos.

4 Escucha y escribe la letra correcta. (1–6)
Escucha otra vez. ¿Positivo 😊 o negativo 😞?

Ejemplo: **1** b 😊

 a   b   c   d   e  f

😊 ¿Qué te gusta?	
Me gusta ♥ Me interesa Me encanta ♥♥	el fútbol la música la natación
Me gustan ♥ Me interesan Me encantan ♥♥	los videojuegos los cómics las hamburguesas

😞 ¿Qué no te gusta?	
No me gusta ✗ Odio ✗✗	la música
No me interesan Odio ✗✗	los cómics

5 Escucha y lee. Copia y rellena la tabla.

Nombre	Jaume Blondi	Pria Fredericks
Edad		
Actividades		
😊		
😞		

b

a

Me llamo Blondi, Jaume Blondi. Soy el agente secreto 00Ñ y soy español. Tengo treinta años. En mi tiempo libre mando mensajes y hago deporte. Me gustan los cómics. Odio las hamburguesas.

Me llamo Pria Fredericks. Soy presentadora de 'Las mañanas con Pria'. Tengo veinticinco años. A ver, en mi tiempo libre escucho música, salgo con mis amigos y voy de compras. Me encantan los videojuegos pero odio el fútbol. ¿Y tú?

6 Con tu compañero/a, pregunta y contesta por Jaume Blondi y Pria Fredericks.

● ¿Cómo te llamas?
■ Me llamo Jaume Blondi.

¿Cómo te llamas?
¿Cuántos años tienes?
¿Qué haces en tu tiempo libre?
¿Qué te gusta?
¿Qué no te gusta?

● Describing friends using adjectives
● Using **y**, **pero**, **también**, **nunca**

 1 Escucha y escribe la letra correcta. (1–10)

Ejemplo: **1** f

¿Cómo es tu mejor amigo?

¿Cómo es tu mejor amiga?

a	b	c	d	e
divertid**o** divertid**a**	hablador hablador**a**	seri**o** seri**a**	perezos**o** perezos**a**	inteligente inteligente
f	g	h	i	j
generos**o** generos**a**	guap**o** guap**a**	alt**o** alt**a**	baj**o** baj**a**	delgad**o** delgad**a**

 2 Escucha y describe a la persona en inglés. (1–6)
Listen and describe the person in English.

Ejemplo: **1** boy – talkative, intelligent, not serious

 3 Escucha otra vez. Escribe la palabra o las palabras del cuadro que entiendes.

Ejemplo: **1** también, no

| y *(and)* | pero *(but)* | no *(not)* | también *(also)* | nunca *(never)* |

 4 Elige cinco personas de tu clase. Tu compañero/a adivina quién es.
Choose five people from your class. Your partner guesses who each person is.

- ● Es una chica.
- ■ ¿Es alta?
- ● No.
- ■ ¿Es generosa?
- ● Sí. Es generosa.
- ■ ¿Es Joanna?

Gramática

masculine sing.	feminine sing.	masculine plural	feminine plural
baj**o**	baja	baj**o**s	baj**a**s
inteligente	inteligente	inteligente**s**	inteligente**s**
hablador	hablador**a***	hablador**es**	hablador**a**s*

*Some adjectives, like **hablador**, add an **-a** for the feminine even though the masculine doesn't end in **-o**.

Para saber más

página 127

5 Escucha y escribe los datos. (1–6)
Listen and note down the details.

Ejemplo: **1** el pelo largo y ondulado

¿Cómo es su pelo?

Tiene el pelo	rubio	negro	pelirrojo	castaño	largo	corto	ondulado

¿De qué color son sus ojos?

Tiene los ojos	marrones	azules	verdes	grises

6 Escucha y lee. Cierra el libro y escribe cinco datos.
Listen and read. Close the book and note down five details.

- ¿Cómo se llama tu mejor amigo?
- ▪ Mi mejor amigo se llama <u>Antonio</u>.
- ¿Cuántos años tiene?
- ▪ Tiene <u>dieciocho años</u>.
- ¿Cómo es?
- ▪ Tiene el pelo <u>corto y castaño</u>. Tiene los ojos <u>marrones</u>. También es <u>alto</u> y <u>delgado</u>.
- ¿Cómo es de carácter?
- ▪ Es <u>divertido</u> y <u>generoso</u> pero nunca es <u>serio</u>.

Gramática

Ser and **tener** are irregular verbs to remember!

ser	**to be**	**tener**	**to have**
soy	*I am*	tengo	*I have*
eres	*you are*	tienes	*you have*
es	*he/she is*	tiene	*he/she has*
somos	*we are*	tenemos	*we have*
sois	*you (plural) are*	tenéis	*you (plural) have*
son	*they are*	tienen	*they have*

Use **tener** for age:
Tengo catorce años.   *I am 14.*

Para saber más   página 130; ej. 6

7 Escribe un diálogo sobre un(a) amigo/a. Utiliza el ejercicio 6 como modelo.
Write a dialogue describing a friend. Use exercise 6 as a model, changing the underlined words.

3 Las estrellas

● Describing celebrities
● Comparing things using **más ... que** *(more ... than)*

Escucha y repite. Escribe las frases en inglés. (1–8)
Listen and repeat. Write the sentences in English.

¿Quién es más alto?

¿Quién es menos alto?

Paco

Alfredo

Sergio

1 Paco es más alto que Alfredo.
2 Alfredo es más alto que Sergio.

3 Alfredo es menos alto que Paco.
4 Sergio es menos alto que Alfredo.

¿Quién es más vieja?   *¿Quién es menos vieja?*

Fabricia

Cristina

Carolina

5 Cristina es más vieja que Fabricia.
6 Carolina es más vieja que Cristina.

7 Cristina es menos vieja que Carolina.
8 Fabricia es menos vieja que Cristina.

¿quién? = *who?*
viejo }
vieja } = *old*

Gramática

Comparatives

más   + adjective + **que**   *more ... than*
menos + adjective + **que**   *less ... than*

Remember, adjectives must agree with the noun they describe.

Para saber más   página 128; ej. 1

Mira las fichas. Escribe frases utilizando 'más ... que' o 'menos ... que'.
Look at the forms. Write sentences using 'more ... than' and 'less ... than'.

Ejemplo: Jennifer Lopez es más vieja
que Eva Longoria.

Nombre: Eva Longoria
Mide: 1,68m
Fecha de nacimiento: el 15 de marzo de 1975

Nombre: Jennifer Lopez
Mide: 1,65m
Fecha de nacimiento: el 24 de julio de 1969

hablar 3 Con tu compañero/a, mira las fotos y las fichas. Pregunta y contesta.

● ¿Quién es más alto, Enrique o Alejandro?
■ Enrique es más alto que Alejandro.

" Remember how to pronounce **j** and **z** in Spanish? Listen and repeat:

*Alejandro San**z** no es vie**j**o, es **j**oven.*
*No es pere**z**oso. **J**uega al a**j**edre**z**.*

joven = *young*
ajedrez = *chess* **"**

Nombre: Enrique Iglesias
Mide: 1,87m
Fecha de nacimiento: el 8 de mayo de 1975

Nombre: Christina Aguilera
Mide: 1,57m
Fecha de nacimiento: el 18 de diciembre de 1980

Nombre: Alejandro Sanz
Mide: 1,70m
Fecha de nacimiento: el 18 de diciembre de 1968

Nombre: Shakira
Mide: 1,52m
Fecha de nacimiento: el 2 de febrero de 1977

¿Enrique o Alejandro?

1 ¿Quién es más alto?
2 ¿Quién es menos guapo?
3 ¿Quién es más viejo?

¿Shakira o Christina?

4 ¿Quién es más guapa?
5 ¿Quién es más joven?
6 ¿Quién es más baja?

escuchar 4 Escucha y rellena los espacios en blanco con las palabras del cuadro.

| alto | perfecto | más | generoso | aburrido | guapo |

Mi mejor amigo

Mi mejor amigo
se llama Rodrigo.
Es (1) ____ y delgado
y más (2) ____ que yo.

Es (3) ____ atractivo
que Ronaldo y Luis Figo.
También es divertido,
nunca es (4) ____ .

Es muy, muy (5) ____ ,
nunca es perezoso.
Le gustan los animales.
Soy su gato, me llamo González.

¡Rodrigo, yo te quiero!
Eres el señor del universo,
totalmente (6) ____ ,
¡mi mejor amigo!

yo te quiero = *I love you*

Mini-test

I can
● introduce myself and talk about activities
● express opinions using **me gusta**
● describe people's character and appearance
G use **ser** and **tener**
G use comparatives

4 Mi rutina diaria

 1 **Escucha y lee el texto.**

¿Qué haces por la mañana?

Por la mañana

 **a** Me despierto.

 **b** Me levanto.

 **c** Me ducho.

 **d** Me peino.

 **e** Me visto.

 **f** Desayuno.

 **g** Voy al instituto.

Gramática

Reflexive verbs describe an action you do to yourself,
e.g. to get yourself up, to shower yourself.

ducharse	*to take a shower*	**despertarse**	*to wake up*
(yo) **me** duch**o**	*I take a shower*	(yo) **me** desp**ie**rt**o**	*I wake up*
(tú) **te** duch**as**	*you take a shower*	(tú) **te** desp**ie**rt**as**	*you wake up*
(él/ella) **se** duch**a**	*he/she/it takes a shower*	(él/ella) **se** desp**ie**rt**a**	*he/she/it wakes up*

Para saber más   página 130; ej. 5

 2 **Haz un sondeo.**
Do a survey.

● ¿Qué haces por la mañana, Isabel?

■ Me peino, desayuno y voy al instituto.

Nombre	Actividades
Isabel	d, f, g

 3 **Escucha y lee.**

¿Qué haces por la tarde?

Por la tarde

  **h** Hago mis deberes.

 **i** Ceno.

 **j** Veo la televisión.

 **k** Me lavo los dientes.

 **l** Me acuesto.

 4 **Escucha y escribe las letras correctas de los ejercicios 1 y 3. (1–5)**

Ejemplo:

1	a, f	h, j

5 **Escucha y lee. Pon los dibujos en el orden del texto.**
Listen and read. Put the drawings into the same order as the text.

Ejemplo: c, …

Normalmente me levanto temprano, me levanto a las nueve de la mañana. Primero me ducho, me lavo los dientes y me peino. ¡Soy muy guapo! Por la mañana juego al fútbol con mi equipo y voy a la sauna. Luego voy a la peluquería. Mi peluquero se llama Rupert y es muy hablador. Después juego con mi ordenador y escucho música. Por la tarde voy al casino con mis amigos. Me encanta jugar al blackjack. También me gusta bailar. Me encantan el hip hop y la música electrónica. Voy a la discoteca, hablo con mucha gente y me acuesto tarde.
Juan Bota de Oro

temprano = *early*

6 **Busca las frases en español en el texto del ejercicio 5. Utiliza la sección Vocabulario.**
Find the Spanish phrases in the exercise 5 text. Use the Vocabulario *section at the end of the book.*

Ejemplo: **1** normally – normalmente

1 normally
2 in the morning
3 then
4 afterwards
5 in the evening
6 also
7 first

7 **Describe tu rutina diaria.**
Use the highlighted phrases in the exercise 5 text.

5 Tu nacionalidad

 1 **Escucha y escribe el nombre correcto. (1–10)**

¿Cuál es tu nacionalidad?

Ejemplo: **1** Meryl

Soy colombiana.

 **Alba**

Soy argentino.

 **Tico**

Soy española.

 **Patricia**

Soy estadounio

Chuck

Soy chilena.

Angélica

Soy galesa.

Meryl

Soy inglés.

Dan

Soy irlandesa.

Margaret

Soy escocés.

Lachlan

Soy mexicano.

Diego

 2 **Juego de memoria.** *Memory game.*

● Soy irlandesa.
■ Eres Margaret.

 3 **Escucha. Copia y rellena la ficha.**

Nombre	*Fernando*
Nacionalidad	
Edad	
☺	
Actividades	
Carácter	
Pelo	
Ojos	

moreno = *dark*
rizado = *curly*

Gramática

masculino	femenino
español	española
inglés	inglesa
escocés	escocesa
irlandés	irlandesa
galés	galesa
mexicano	mexicana
colombiano	colombiana
argentino	argentina
chileno	chilena
estadounidense	estadounidense

Para saber más **página 127**

4 Con tu compañero/a, lee y completa el diálogo por Lola.

Nombre	Lola
Nacionalidad	estadounidense
Edad	13

Actividades

Carácter	divertida, habladora
Pelo	rubio, largo
Ojos	marrones

- ¿Cómo te llamas?
- ■ Me llamo _____
- ¿Cuál es tu nacionalidad?
- ■ Soy _____
- ¿Cuántos años tienes?
- ■ Tengo _____
- ¿Qué te gusta?
- ■ Me gusta _____
- ¿Qué haces en tu tiempo libre?
- ■ En mi tiempo libre _____
- ¿Cómo eres?
- ■ Soy _____
- ¿Cómo es tu pelo?
- ■ Tengo el pelo _____
- ¿De qué color son tus ojos?
- ■ Tengo _____

 5 Lee el texto y contesta a las preguntas en inglés.

¡Hola! Me llamo Gerardo. Soy colombiano. Tengo catorce años. Vivo en Bogotá. Es la capital de Colombia y es una ciudad muy importante. Me gusta mucho.

Me encantan los videojuegos y el fútbol. Normalmente juego al fútbol en el parque con mis amigos. También juego en un equipo del instituto. Mañana voy a jugar un partido. En mi tiempo libre, juego con el ordenador o salgo con mis amigos. No escucho música. ¡Nunca voy de compras! ¡Qué aburrido!

Tengo los ojos marrones y el pelo corto y marrón. Tengo gafas. Soy más alto que mi hermana Silvia, pero menos alto que mi hermano Rodrigo. Soy inteligente pero un poco perezoso. No me gustan los deberes.

Mi rutina diaria es muy aburrida. Por la mañana me despierto, me levanto y me ducho. ¡No me peino! Desayuno y luego voy al instituto. Por la tarde hago mis deberes, ceno y veo la televisión un poco. Me acuesto a las diez. ¡Buenas noches!

1 Give Gerardo's nationality and age.
2 Give two details about Bogotá.
3 What pastimes does Gerardo like?
4 What does he say about football?
5 What does Gerardo do in his free time?
6 What does he look like? Give four details.
7 How does he describe his personality?
8 Describe his daily routine
  a) in the morning and
  b) in the afternoon.

6 Escribe una respuesta a Gerardo.
Write a reply to Gerardo.

- *Answer the questions in exercise 4.*
- *Describe your daily routine.*
- *Use connectives:* y, pero, también, …
- *Use time expressions:* normalmente, nunca, …

To reach a higher level, try to add something about the future.

Mañana **voy a** { jugar al fútbol.
ir de compras.
hacer deporte.

Resumen

Unidad 1

I can

- say what I do in my free time
- express opinions

- **G** use regular verbs in the present tense
- **G** use irregular verbs in the present tense

Mando mensajes. Bailo.
Me gusta la música.
Me interesan los videojuegos.
Chateo por internet.
Voy de compras. Hago deporte.
Salgo con mis amigos.

Unidad 2

I can

- ask what someone's best friend is like

- describe someone's character
- describe someone's appearance

- **G** use connectives
- **G** use negatives
- **G** recognise the present tense forms of **tener** and **ser**

¿Cómo es tu mejor amigo?
¿Cómo es tu mejor amiga?
Es divertida y habladora.
Tiene el pelo corto y castaño.
Tiene los ojos marrones.
Es alto y delgado.
Es divertido **y también** generoso.
No es perezoso. **Nunca** es serio.
Antonio **tiene** dieciocho años.
Tiene el pelo corto y castaño.
Es bajo y guapo.

Unidad 3

I can

- **G** use **¿quién?** (who?) to ask questions about people
- **G** use comparatives

¿Quién es más guapa, Shakira o Christina?
Alfredo es **más** alto **que** Sergio.
Fabricia es **menos** alta **que** Carolina.

Unidad 4

I can

- describe my daily routine
- ask about someone's routine

- use sequencing words

- **G** use reflexive verbs

Por la mañana desayuno, voy al instituto …
¿Qué haces por la mañana?
¿Qué haces por la tarde?
Normalmente me levanto a las siete.
Primero me ducho y **luego** me peino.
me levanto, me ducho, me peino

Unidad 5

I can

- give my nationality
- understand nationalities
- **G** use connectives
- **G** make nationality adjectives agree

Soy inglés. Soy galesa.
español, escocesa, mexicana, estadounidense
y, pero, también
Diego es mexicano. Alba es colombiana.

1 Escucha. ¿Quién habla? ¿Paco o Pepe?

Paco

Pepe

2 Con tu compañero/a, haz diálogos.

- ¿Cuál es tu nacionalidad?
- Soy <u>escocés</u>.
- ¿Cómo eres?
- Soy <u>generoso</u> y <u>divertido</u>.

3 Escribe los nombres correctos.

Ejemplo: **a** Andrea

Gloria es más alta que Andrea pero menos alta que Raquel.
Letizia es más alta que Raquel pero menos alta que Belén.

4 Escribe frases.

Ejemplo: Por la mañana me despierto.

Por la mañana ...

Por la tarde ...

¡Extra! 1

- Using frequency words
- Practising reflexive verbs

escuchar 1 Escucha y apunta las respuestas de Alba y Tico.

Ejemplo: **1** Alba a – Tico c

siempre	*always*
a menudo	*often*
a veces	*sometimes*
de vez en cuando	*from time to time*
nunca	*never*

¿Eres interesante o no?

Elige una opción y calcula para obtener el resultado del test.

1 Bailas en la discoteca …
- **a** siempre
- **b** a menudo
- **c** a veces
- **d** de vez en cuando
- **e** nunca

2 Te acuestas muy tarde …
- **a** siempre
- **b** a menudo
- **c** a veces
- **d** de vez en cuando
- **e** nunca

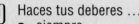
tarde = *late*

3 Haces tus deberes …
- **a** siempre
- **b** a menudo
- **c** a veces
- **d** de vez en cuando
- **e** nunca

4 Te levantas tarde …
- **a** nunca
- **b** de vez en cuando
- **c** a veces
- **d** a menudo
- **e** siempre

5 Haces deporte …
- **a** siempre
- **b** a menudo
- **c** a veces
- **d** de vez en cuando
- **e** nunca

6 Vas de compras …
- **a** siempre
- **b** a menudo
- **c** a veces
- **d** de vez en cuando
- **e** nunca

7 Comes hamburguesas …
- **a** nunca
- **b** de vez en cuando
- **c** a veces
- **d** a menudo
- **e** siempre

8 Chateas por internet …
- **a** siempre
- **b** a menudo
- **c** a veces
- **d** de vez en cuando
- **e** nunca

9 Lees cómics …
- **a** siempre
- **b** a menudo
- **c** a veces
- **d** de vez en cuando
- **e** nunca

10 En una fiesta eres la persona más habladora …
- **a** siempre
- **b** a menudo
- **c** a veces
- **d** de vez en cuando
- **e** nunca

¡Ahora calcula!
- **a** = 5 puntos
- **b** = 4 puntos
- **c** = 3 puntos
- **d** = 2 puntos
- **e** = 1 punto

10–25 puntos: ¡Qué aburrido/a eres! ¿Tienes amigos? ¡Imposible! Es bueno hacer cosas diferentes y divertidas. Intenta salir una vez por semana.

26–40 puntos: Eres interesante pero un poco perezoso/a. Te gustan cosas diferentes como bailar o leer, pero te encanta dormir.

41–50 puntos: Necesitas días de 25 horas. Te gusta salir, te encantan las fiestas y además estudias mucho. ¡Eres muy interesante!

hablar 2 Con tu compañero/a, pregunta y contesta:
haz el test del ejercicio 1.

3 Escribe un texto: describe tus pasatiempos, utilizando el test como modelo.

Ejemplo: En la discoteca siempre bailo.
        Me acuesto a menudo muy tarde.

4 Lee el texto y escribe la letra o las letras correctas.

Ejemplo: **1** a

> mi vida = *my life*
> agradable = *pleasant*
> atún = *tuna*
> después de … = *after …ing*

Abajo

b   el salón

c   la terraza

d   la cocina

e   el comedor

Arriba

el dormitorio

f

g

el cuarto de baño

h   i   j

1 ¡Hola! Me llamo Kiki. Vivo en una casa pequeña en un pueblo con mi madre. Mi vida es muy agradable. Soy inteligente, pero un poco perezosa.

2 A ver … Por la mañana me despierto y me levanto.

3 Luego desayuno en la terraza. Después me lavo los dientes en la cocina.

4 Veo la televisión abajo en el salón. En mi tiempo libre, escucho música y voy de compras también. Me encanta la música pero odio el fútbol. No me interesa.

5 Por la tarde me ducho en el cuarto de baño. Me peino también. Tengo el pelo rizado y los ojos marrones.

6 Me visto para cenar. Ceno con mi madre en el comedor. Me gustan los bocadillos de atún.

7 Después de cenar, me acuesto.

5 Lee el texto otra vez. Contesta a las preguntas en español.

1 ¿Cómo es Kiki de carácter?
2 ¿Qué hace en su tiempo libre?
3 ¿Qué le gusta?
4 ¿Cómo es su pelo?
5 ¿De qué color son sus ojos?

¡Extra! 2

escuchar 1 Escucha y lee.

1

D – Lo siento.
P – Lo siento.
D – ¡Hola! Me llamo Diego. **Soy** español.
   Mucho gusto, mucho gusto …

2

D – ¿Cómo te llamas? ¿Cuál es tu
   nacionalidad?
P – Me llamo Patricia. Soy mexicana
   pero **vivo** en Barcelona.

3

D – Yo también vivo en Barcelona. ¿Y te gusta
   Barcelona, Patricia?
P – ¡Ah sí, me encanta, me encanta! Es una
   ciudad muy interesante y muy importante
   también, porque es la capital de Cataluña. Me
   gustan los monumentos y las galerías de arte.

4

D – ¿Qué **haces** en tu tiempo libre, Patricia?
P – Me encanta la música. **Escucho** de todo.
   Me gusta bailar.

5

P – ¿Y tú? ¿Qué haces en tu tiempo libre?
D – **Chateo** por internet. Me gustan los videojuegos.
   Juego con el ordenador y **mando** mensajes.
   Me gusta mucho la informática. Aquí tienes mi
   correo electrónico.

6

P – ¡Hola Ana! ¿Qué tal?
   Conocí a un chico hoy. Es alto y delgado.
   Tiene el pelo castaño y los ojos azules …

lo siento = I'm sorry
mucho gusto = pleased to meet you
conocí a = I got to know
hoy = today

2 Con tu compañero/a, lee en voz alta la historia de Diego y Patricia.
With your partner, read the story of Diego and Patricia aloud.

 3 Escribe los infinitivos de los verbos de la historia. Luego escríbelos en inglés.
Write the infinitives of the verbs in orange in the story. Then write them in English.

Present tense	Infinitive
soy = I am	ser = to be

 4 Lee la historia otra vez y escribe Diego (D), Patricia (P) o Diego y Patricia (DP).

1 ¿Quién es español?
2 ¿Quién es mexicana?
3 ¿Quién vive en Barcelona?
4 ¿Quién tiene el pelo castaño y los ojos azules?
5 ¿Quién juega con el ordenador?
6 ¿Quién escucha música y baila en su tiempo libre?

 5 Imagina otra historia de dos personas que se encuentran en Barcelona.
Incluye estas expresiones.
Make up another story about two people who meet in Barcelona. Include these expressions.

- Lo siento.
- Mucho gusto.
- ¿Cómo te llamas?
- ¿Cuántos años tienes?
- ¿Qué te gusta?
- ¿Qué haces en tu tiempo libre?

 6 Escucha el texto de Zona Cultura.

> Colón = (Christopher) Columbus
> cafetería = café
> catalán = Catalan (a language spoken in Catalonia and in parts of France and Sardinia)

Barcelona

Barcelona está en el noreste de España. Es una ciudad muy importante.

Hay monumentos interesantes, galerías de arte y muchos restaurantes y cafeterías.

Barcelona es la capital de la región de Cataluña. En Cataluña se habla catalán.

Las Ramblas

Plaza de Cataluña

Monumento a Colón

Palabras

En mi tiempo libre
¿Qué haces en tu
tiempo libre?
Bailo.
Chateo por internet.
Escucho música.
Hago deporte.
Juego con el
ordenador.
Mando mensajes.
Salgo con mis amigos.

Voy de compras.

¿Qué te gusta?
Me gusta …
Me interesa …
Me encanta …
el fútbol
la música
la natación
Me gustan …
Me interesan …
Me encantan …
los cómics
los videojuegos
las hamburguesas

¿Qué no te gusta?
No me gusta la música.
Odio el fútbol.
No me interesan los
cómics.

Los amigos
tu mejor amigo/a
¿Cómo es?

Es …
alto/a
bajo/a
delgado/a
guapo/a

In my free time
*What do you do in
your free time?*
I dance.
I chat online.
I listen to music.
I do sport.
I play on my computer.

I send messages.
*I go out with my
friends.*
I go shopping.

What do you like?
I like …
I'm interested in …
I love …
football
music
swimming
I like …
I'm interested in …
I love …
comics
video games
hamburgers

What don't you like?
I don't like music.
I hate football.
*I'm not interested in
comics.*

Friends
your best friend
*What is he/she like?,
What does he/she
look like?*
He/She is …
tall
short
slim
*good-looking,
attractive*

¿Cómo es de carácter?

Es …
No es …
Nunca es …
divertido/a
generoso/a
hablador(a)
inteligente
perezoso/a
serio/a

¿Cómo es su pelo?
Tiene el pelo …
castaño
negro
pelirrojo
rubio
corto
largo
ondulado

¿De qué color son
sus ojos?
Tiene los ojos …
azules
grises
marrones
verdes

Más o menos
¿Quién es más alto/a?
¿Quién es menos alto/a?
… es más viejo/a que …
… es menos joven
que …

*What kind of person is
he/she?*
He/She is …
He/She isn't …
He/She is never …
amusing
generous
talkative, chatty
intelligent
lazy
serious

What is his/her hair like?
He/She has … hair.
brown
black
red
fair, blond
short
long
wavy

*What colour are his/her
eyes?*
He/She has … eyes.
blue
grey
brown
green

More or less
Who is taller?
Who is less tall/shorter?
… is older than …
*… is less young than/
isn't as young as …*

Mi rutina diaria	*My daily routine*
¿Qué haces por la mañana?	*What do you do in the morning?*
Por la mañana …	*In the morning …*
me despierto	*I wake up*
me levanto	*I get up*
me ducho	*I shower*
me peino	*I comb/brush my hair*
me visto	*I get dressed*
desayuno	*I have breakfast*
voy al instituto	*I go to school*
¿Qué haces por la tarde?	*What do you do in the evening?*
Por la tarde …	*In the evening …*
hago mis deberes	*I do my homework*
ceno	*I have dinner/supper*
veo la televisión	*I watch TV*
me lavo los dientes	*I brush my teeth*
me acuesto	*I go to bed*
¿Cuándo?	*When?*
después	*afterwards*
luego	*then*
normalmente	*normally*
por la mañana	*in the morning*
por la tarde	*in the evening*
primero	*first*
Nacionalidades	*Nationalities*
¿Cuál es tu nacionalidad?	*What is your nationality?*
Soy …	*I'm …*
argentino/a	*Argentinian*
chileno/a	*Chilean*
colombiano/a	*Colombian*
escocés/escocesa	*Scottish*
español(a)	*Spanish*
estadounidense	*American*
galés/galesa	*Welsh*
inglés/inglesa	*English*
irlandés/irlandesa	*Irish*
mexicano/a	*Mexican*

Palabras muy útiles	*Very useful words*
nunca	*never*
pero	*but*
también	*also*
y	*and*
o	*or*
más	*more*
menos	*less*
mejor	*better, best*

Estrategia

Building your vocabulary

Try to collect words so that you can use them again. Here are some ideas:

1 Note down words in different categories:
   Verbs
   Adjectives
   Nouns
   Cognates

2 Note down words under different topic headings:
   Hobbies
   Daily routine
   Appearance
   Character
   Opinions

3 Note down words as pairs of opposites:
   alto/a – bajo/a

4 If you find a word difficult to remember, write out a sentence using it:
   lazy = perezoso
   Mi mejor amigo es inteligente, pero un poco **perezoso**.

escuchar **1** Escucha y escribe la letra correcta. (1–8)

Ejemplo: **1** f

¿Adónde vas?

¿Qué vas a **hacer**?

a

Voy al cine.
Voy a **ver** una película.

b

Voy al parque.
Voy a **jugar** al fútbol.

c

Voy al centro comercial.
Voy a **ir** de compras.

d

Voy al estadio.
Voy a **ver** un partido de fútbol.

e

Voy al salón recreativo.
Voy a **jugar** al futbolín.

f

Voy a la playa.
Voy a **tomar** el sol.

g

Voy a la bolera.
Voy a **jugar** a los bolos.

h

Voy a la discoteca.
Voy a **bailar**.

salón recreativo = *amusement arcade*

escribir **2** Escribe una lista de los **infinitivos** del ejercicio 1. Luego escríbelos en inglés.

Ejemplo: hacer = to do

Gramática

If **a** (to) and **el** come together, they join up to make **al**.

Voy **al** estadio.
Voy **a la** playa.

Para saber más página 135

3 Elige un sitio.
Tu compañero/a dice
la actividad.
*Choose a place. Your partner
says the activity.*

- Voy al cine.
- Vas a ver una película.

Gramática

The near future tense

ir *(to go)*

voy a	
vas a	
va a	bailar
vamos a	
vais a	
van a	

Voy a **bailar**.
I'm going to dance.
¿Qué vas a **hacer**?
What are you going to do?
Vamos a **ver** un partido de fútbol.
We're going to see a football match.

Para saber más   página 131 ex. 9

4 Escucha a Milena. Copia y rellena la tabla. (1–6)

Día	Sitio(s)	Actividad(es)
lunes	parque	fútbol

5 Lee el texto y mira los dibujos.
¿Verdadero o falso? Escribe V o F.

Ejemplo: **1** F

La semana de Sergio

El lunes   Voy a tomar el
sol y jugar al voleibol en la
playa con mis amigos. Me
gusta mucho.

El martes   Voy a ver un
partido de fútbol en la
televisión. ¡Qué guay! Me
encanta el fútbol. Mi equipo
preferido es el Barça y
Ronaldinho es mi jugador
favorito. No me gusta nada el
Real Madrid.

El miércoles Voy a ver una
película de horror con
una amiga. Va a ser muy
divertido. Me encantan las
películas de horror, pero
no me gustan las películas
románticas.

El jueves   Voy a salir con
mis amigos. Vamos a
bailar en una discoteca
en el centro comercial.
La discoteca se llama
Ritmotrón.

El viernes   No voy a ir de
compras porque no me
gusta nada. Pero voy a
jugar con mi ordenador.
Tengo un juego nuevo
que se llama 'Los cuatro
fantásticos'. ¡Es estupendo!

El sábado   Voy a jugar
al futbolín en el salón
recreativo con mi mejor
amigo Paco. ¡Por supuesto,
voy a ganar!

El domingo

6 Describe tu semana ideal. Da opiniones.

Ejemplo: El lunes no voy a ir al instituto. Voy a …

 **Escucha y lee.**

1 ¡Hola! Me llamo Estela Estrella. Soy una gran estrella. Normalmente no me levanto de la cama por menos de 40 millones de dólares … Hoy es un día normal para mí.

¿Qué vas a hacer hoy?

2 *Esta mañana no* voy a salir.

3 *Primero* voy a ver la televisión …

4 … y *luego* voy a escuchar música.

5 *Esta tarde* voy a salir a las dos.

6 *Después* voy a ir al balneario por la tarde …

7 … y *más tarde* voy a ir a la peluquería.

8 *Esta noche* voy a ir al casino …

9 … y *por último* a la discoteca. Voy a bailar toda la noche. ¡Va a ser muy divertido!

 Busca el equivalente en español en los textos.

Ejemplo: **1** después

1 afterwards	**4** this evening	**7** tonight
2 first	**5** then	**8** finally
3 this morning	**6** later	

> cama = *bed*
> por menos de = *for less than*
> hoy = *today*
> va a ser = *it's going to be*

3 **Con tu compañero/a, haz dos diálogos utilizando estos dibujos.**

● ¿Qué vas a hacer hoy?
■ Esta mañana no voy a salir. Primero …

> Listen to the double vowel sound **ue** and practise saying it.
>
> Los j**ue**ves escucho música. Desp**ué**s j**ue**go al futbolín y l**ue**go me ac**ue**sto …

a esta mañana   primero   luego

b esta tarde   más tarde   después

4 Escucha y lee. Luego corrige las frases en inglés.

Ejemplo: **1** Normally Ramón chats on the internet and doesn't go out much.

Ramón

Generalmente chateo por internet y no salgo mucho, pero hoy voy a ver un partido de fútbol muy especial, un partido internacional: España e Italia. Va a ser muy, muy divertido y el equipo español va a ganar (¡espero!).

Después, voy a ir al salón recreativo con mis amigos y vamos a jugar al futbolín un rato. Más tarde vamos a ir a la discoteca y vamos a bailar.

Mireya

Generalmente los fines de semana juego con el ordenador o escucho música pero este fin de semana voy a hacer otra cosa. Es un fin de semana especial porque es el cumpleaños de mi mejor amiga, Susa.

Primero vamos a ir de compras, luego vamos a ir al balneario juntas y después a la peluquería. Más tarde vamos a ir a la bolera y vamos a jugar a los bolos.

1 Normally Ramón listens to music and doesn't go out much.
2 He is going to see an international volleyball game.
3 It is going to be very boring.
4 Afterwards he is going to play pinball.
5 Mireya is going to go shopping with her sister.
6 Then they are going to go swimming.
7 Afterwards they are going to go to the cinema.
8 Later on they are going to watch TV.

Gramática

Get into the habit of checking what tense a verb is in. Look again at Ramón's and Mireya's texts and make two lists of the verbs.

Presente	Futuro
chateo	voy a ver

Para saber más página 133; ej. 13

5 Describe un fin de semana para Cenicienta.

Los fines de semana (un verbo en el presente) ...
pero este fin de semana (un verbo en el futuro) ...
Luego (un verbo en el futuro) ...
y después (otro verbo en el futuro) ...
Más tarde (otro
verbo en el futuro) ...

3 ¿Te gustaría ir a la bolera?

 1 Escucha y lee el diálogo.

Susa: Hola Rico, ¿qué tal?
Rico: Muy bien, ¿y tú?
Susa: Muy bien. Oye, ¿te gustaría ir al estadio el jueves?
Rico: Muy bien. ¿A qué hora?
Susa: Bueno … a las tres.
Rico: ¿Dónde quedamos?
Susa: Delante del estadio.
Rico: Hasta luego.
Susa: Hasta luego.

> **¿Te gustaría …?** *(Would you like to …?)* is very useful for inviting people to do something. Like **Voy a …**, it's always followed by an infinitive.

 2 Escucha y rellena la tabla en inglés. (1–6)

	Place to go/activity	Day	Time to meet	Place to meet
1	bowling alley	Tuesday	6:45	in bowling alley

¿Te gustaría ir	al parque?
♥	al estadio?
	al salón recreativo?
	a la bolera?
	a la discoteca?
	de compras?
¿A qué hora?	A las tres
	A las cinco y media
	A las seis y cuarto
	A las siete menos cuarto
	A las ocho
	A las nueve
¿Dónde quedamos?	Delante de la discoteca
	Detrás del centro comercial
	En el parque
	En la bolera
	En la calle
	En tu casa

Gramática

en	in
a	to
delante de	in front of
detrás de	behind

a + el = **al**
de + el = **del**

Para saber más   página 135

Escuchar 3 Escucha otra vez. Escribe las frases que entiendes.

Listen again. Write down the phrases you hear.

De acuerdo.
Vale.
Muy bien.

No tengo ganas.
¡Ni hablar!
¡Ni en sueños!

Bueno …
Pues …
A ver …

Hasta luego.
Adiós.
Hasta pronto.

Hablar 4 Con tu compañero/a, haz cuatro diálogos. Utiliza las frases de los ejercicios 2 y 3.

martes

domingo

viernes

sábado

Leer 5 Lee el texto y dibuja 😊 o 🙁 para cada actividad.

1   2   3   4

---

miespacio.com

● **miespacio**   *El lugar de los amigos*

| Vídeos | Favoritos | Foros | Grupos | Música |

Chicachica

chica
16 años
Badalona
Última entrada:
4/10/08

Chicachica	¡Hola Luluazul! ¿Te gustaría ir a la bolera el viernes a las ocho?
Luluazul	¡Ni en sueños! Odio jugar a los bolos. No me gusta nada.
Chicachica	A ver, entonces, ¿quieres ir al cine? ¿Te gustaría ver una película?
Luluazul	No, Chicachica, no tengo ganas.
Chicachica	Bueno, ¿te gustaría ir al salón recreativo? Vamos a jugar al futbolín.
Luluazul	¡Ni hablar! No me gusta nada jugar al futbolín.
Chicachica	¿Qué vamos a hacer entonces?
Luluazul	¿Te gustaría ir a la discoteca?
Chicachica	Síííííííí, me encanta bailar. ¿Dónde quedamos?
Luluazul	En tu casa a las nueve.
Chicachica	Muy bien. ¡Hasta luego, Luluazul! Je je. 😊

Escribir 6 Escribe un diálogo entre dos personas chateando. Utiliza el ejercicio 5 como modelo.

Mini-test

I can
● say where I am going in town
● say what I am going to do using the near future tense
● use sequencing words (**primero, después, …**)
● use the near future and present tenses together
● invite someone to go out

4 No puedo . . .

● Making excuses
● Using **querer** and **poder**

escuchar 1 Escucha. ¿Quién habla? Escribe el nombre. (1–8)

 ¿Quieres salir?

 No, …

Ejemplo: **1** Antonio

 Tengo que hacer mis deberes.

Carolina

 Tengo que ordenar mi dormitorio.

Sergio

 Tengo que pasear al perro.

Antonio

 Tengo que lavarme el pelo.

Rosa

 No quiero.

Sergio

No tengo dinero.

Eduardo

 No tengo tiempo.

María

 Lo siento, no puedo.

Alejandro

escuchar 2 Escucha y rellena la tabla en inglés. (1–6)

	Activity	Excuse
1	football	has to walk dog

Gramática

tener = *to have*
tener que + **infinitive** = *to have to*

Tengo un perro.   *I have a dog.*
Tengo que **pasear** al perro.   *I have to walk the dog.*

Para saber más   **página 130; ej. 7**

hablar 3 Con tu compañero/a, haz diálogos.

● ¿Quieres <u>ver un partido de fútbol</u>?
■ Lo siento, no puedo.
● ¿Por qué?
■ Porque <u>no tengo tiempo</u>.

 ¿por qué? = *why?*
porque = *because*

¿Quieres …?	ir a la discoteca
	ir de compras
	chatear por internet
No puedo	ver un partido de fútbol
	ver una película
	jugar a los bolos
	jugar al fútbol

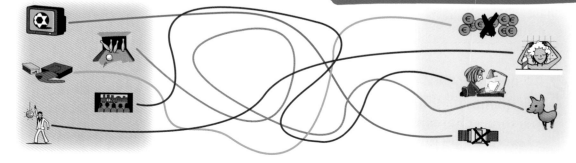

Gramática

Poder and **querer** are stem-changing verbs. They are usually followed by an **infinitive**.

querer	*to want*	poder	*to be able to/'can'*
qu**ie**ro	*I want*	p**ue**do	*I can*
qu**ie**res	*you want*	p**ue**des	*you can*
qu**ie**re	*he/she wants*	p**ue**de	*he/she can*
queremos	*we want*	podemos	*we can*
queréis	*you (plural) want*	podéis	*you (plural) can*
qu**ie**ren	*they want*	p**ue**den	*they can*

¿Quieres **salir**? *Do you want to go out?* | No puedo **salir**. *I can't go out.*

Para saber más página 129; ej. 4

 4 Escucha y canta.

 5 Busca estas frases en español en la canción.

Ejemplo: **1** No, no puedo.

1 No, I can't.
2 I hate the cinema.
3 No, I don't want to.
4 I'm sorry.
5 I haven't any money.
6 I have to tidy the lounge.

> hace viento = *it's windy*
> sólo = *only*
> pastel = *cake*

¿Por qué?

¿Por qué siempre me dices 'no'?
'No, no puedo',
'No, no quiero',
'No tengo dinero'.

 ¿Te gustaría ir a la playa
el lunes por la noche?
'Creo que no, lo siento,
porque hoy hace mucho viento.'

 ¿Quieres ver una peli
el martes a las cuatro?
'Lo siento, odio el cine.
Sólo me gusta el teatro.'

 ¿Este fin de semana
quieres ir a la bolera?
'No, quiero ver la televisión
y tengo que ordenar el salón.'

 ¿Te gustaría ir de compras
el miércoles a las tres?
'No tengo dinero, pero vale,
si me compras un pastel.'

 6 No quieres salir. Inventa la excusa más larga.
You don't want to go out. Make up the longest excuse you can.

Ejemplo: No puedo salir. Tengo que lavarme el pelo y después pasear al perro …
y luego … después … más tarde …

5 Tengo un problema

escuchar 1 Escucha y lee.

Sergio: Mamá, me gustaría ir al concierto de Shakira y luego a la discoteca. ¿Tienes 20 euros?

Mamá: Pero Sergio, hoy vamos a la ópera. Tu hermana es la cantante principal.

Sergio: Mamá, ¡ni en sueños! No me gusta nada la ópera. Es muy aburrida. No puedo ir. Sólo me gusta la música moderna. Quiero salir con mis amigos y bailar. Me gusta mucho bailar.

Mamá: Lo siento, Sergio, pero tienes que ir a la ópera.

Sergio: Mamá, por favor, odio hacer cosas en casa, pero esta semana voy a ordenar el dormitorio y también voy a hacer mis deberes.

Mamá: Eso es fantástico, en tal caso puedes …

Sergio: ¡Qué guay! ¡Gracias, mamá!

Mamá: … hacer los deberes ahora, pero tienes que ir a la ópera luego.

Sergio: Pero mamá, por favor …

> concierto = *concert*
> cantante = *singer*
> sólo me gusta = *I only like*
> cosas en casa = *things at home*
> en tal caso = *in that case*

> What do all these expressions have in common?
>
> Me gusta …   (*I like …*)
> Me gustaría … (*I would like to …*)
> Tienes que …   (*You have to …*)
> Tengo que …   (*I have to …*)
> Quiero …   (*I want to …*)
> Voy a …   (*I am going to …*)
>
> They are all followed by an **infinitive**.

hablar 2 Con tu compañero/a, lee el diálogo.

Gramática

To say that someone likes or dislikes something, use **le**.

Le gusta bailar.   *He/She likes to dance.*
No **le** gusta la ópera.   *He/She doesn't like opera.*

To make it clear who you are talking about, add **a** + the person's name.

A Sergio le gusta ir a la discoteca.   *Sergio likes to go to the disco.*
A Sergio no le gusta hacer los deberes. *Sergio doesn't like to do homework.*

Para saber más   **página 134; ej. 16**

hablar 3 Con tu compañero/a, pregunta y contesta.

● ¿A Sergio le gusta la ópera?
■ No, no le gusta nada la ópera.

1 ¿A Sergio le gusta la ópera?
2 ¿Qué tipo de música le gusta?
3 ¿Le gusta bailar?
4 ¿Qué cosas no le gusta hacer?
5 ¿Le gusta ir a la discoteca?

Empareja los problemas con los consejos de Tatiana.
Match up the problems with Tatiana's advice. (There is one solution too many.)

Los consejos de Tatiana ...

1 Tatiana, tengo un problema. Mi hermano, para su cumpleaños, va a jugar a los bolos con sus amigos. Yo tengo que ir, pero no tengo ganas. ¡No es justo! Odio jugar a los bolos. ¡Es muy, muy aburrido! ¿Qué voy a hacer?
Juana, Bilbao

2 Generalmente, no salgo mucho. No me gusta nada. Prefiero jugar con el ordenador o ver la televisión. También me gusta hacer mis deberes y escuchar música en mi dormitorio. Mis padres dicen que tengo que salir más, pero no quiero …
Pepe, Almagro

3 Me encanta el fútbol y el sábado quiero ver un partido de fútbol en el centro. Mi madre dice que no puedo ir porque soy demasiado joven. Pero quiero ir con un amigo que tiene dieciocho años. Es un amigo muy responsable. ¿Qué le puedo decir a mi madre?
Javier, Madrid

a Estoy de acuerdo con tu padre – eres demasiado joven para ir a la discoteca.

b Tienes que pensar en tu hermano. Es su día especial. Tienes que salir con él.

c Tienes que presentar el amigo a tu madre. Tu madre puede decidir si él es responsable o no.

d Tu vida es un poco triste. Tienes que salir más. No es sano pasar tanto tiempo en tu dormitorio.

demasiado = *too*
sano = *healthy*
pasar = *to spend*
tanto tiempo = *so much time*

 Lee los textos otra vez. Busca estas frases en español.

1 What am I going to do?
2 My parents say that I have to go out more.
3 Your life is a bit sad.
4 What can I tell my mother?
5 It's not fair!
6 I have a problem.
7 I agree with your father.
8 You are too young.

Gramática

Possessive adjectives

Like other adjectives, these change to agree with singular and plural nouns.

	singular	plural
my	mi ⎫	mi**s** ⎫
your	tu ⎬ hermano	tu**s** ⎬ padre**s**
his/her	su ⎭	su**s** ⎭

Para saber más   página 128

 Describe un problema. Utiliza los textos como modelos.

Resumen

Unidad 1

I can

- ■ name places in town — la bolera, el estadio, el parque, …
- ■ ask someone where they are going — ¿Adónde vas?
- ■ say where I am going — Voy al centro comercial. Voy a la playa.
- G use the near future tense — Voy a ver una película. Voy a tomar el sol.
- G recognise infinitives in Spanish — jugar, hacer, ir, …

Unidad 2

I can

- ■ pronounce two vowels together — **lue**go me ac**ue**sto
- G use sequencing words — **Primero** voy a ver la televisión y **luego** voy a escuchar música. **Esta tarde** voy a salir a las dos.
- G use the present and near future tenses together — Generalmente, los fines de semana **juego** con el ordenador, pero hoy **voy a salir** con una amiga.

Unidad 3

I can

- ■ invite someone to go out — ¿Te gustaría ir al estadio el jueves?
- ■ arrange a time — ¿A qué hora? A las tres.
- ■ arrange a place to meet — ¿Dónde quedamos? Delante del estadio.
- ■ use filler phrases — A ver …, Pues …, Bueno …
- ■ say that I agree — De acuerdo. Vale. Muy bien.
- G use prepositions — **delante del** centro comercial, **detrás de** la discoteca, **en** la bolera

Unidad 4

I can

- ■ turn down an invitation — Lo siento, no puedo.
- ■ make an excuse — No tengo dinero.
- G use **tener que** + infinitive — Tengo que ordenar mi dormitorio.
- G use **querer** + infinitive — No quiero salir. Quiero ver la televisión.
- G use **poder** + infinitive — No puedo jugar al fútbol.

Unidad 5

I can

- ■ talk about what other people like — A Sergio le gusta bailar.
- G understand phrases with infinitives — Tengo que …, No quiero …, Me gustaría …, Voy a …
- G understand singular and plural possessive adjectives — **mis** padres, **su** día especial, **tu** madre

1 Escucha. Copia y rellena la tabla. (1–5)

	What?	When?	Where?
1	football match	Thursday	in front of stadium

 2 Con tu compañero/a, haz diálogos.

- ● ¿Quieres <u>ir a la bolera</u>?
- ■ Lo siento, no puedo. <u>Tengo que pasear al perro</u>.

 3 Pon los dibujos en el orden correcto del texto.

Ejemplo: d, ...

a   **b**   **c**   **d**   **e**   **f**

Jorge

> Normalmente, los fines de semana juego al fútbol en el parque con mis amigos, pero este fin de semana no voy a jugar al fútbol. Voy a ir al estadio y voy a ver un partido de fútbol: Real Madrid y Valencia.
>
> Habitualmente no hago mis deberes, pero el domingo no voy a salir. Voy a estudiar porque tengo exámenes el lunes. Después voy a chatear un poco por internet y luego voy a escuchar música. Me gusta mucho la música cubana. También me gusta mucho jugar con el ordenador y voy a jugar un rato si tengo tiempo.

 4 Copia y rellena la tabla con los verbos en presente o futuro del ejercicio 3.

Presente	Futuro
juego	no voy a jugar

 5 Describe tu semana. Utiliza las palabras del cuadro (*sequencing words*).

Ejemplo: El lunes voy a ir de compras y luego voy a ir al parque. ...

primero   luego   después   más tarde   por la mañana   por la tarde

escuchar 1 **Escucha y lee.**

Make a list of cognates in the brochure text.

Ejemplo: el parque = park

El parque de atracciones de Calella

¿Quieres explorar el mundo perdido del jurásico?

¿Te gustaría tomar el tren minero?

¿Te interesa practicar las artes circenses?

¿Vas a navegar por los rápidos del Río Rojo?

¿Quieres montar en la montaña rusa?

leer 2 **Busca los infinitivos en el texto del ejercicio 1. Escríbelos en inglés.**

Ejemplo: explorar = to explore

escuchar 3 **Escucha el diálogo y pon los dibujos en el orden correcto.**

Ejemplo: d, …

 a
 b
 c
 d
 e

4 Escucha otra vez. Haz una lista de las opiniones que entiendes.

Ejemplo: me gustaría mucho

 5 Con tu compañero/a, planea un día en el parque de atracciones.

- ● ¿Primero vamos a …?
- ■ Sí, de acuerdo. ¿A qué hora?
- ● A las …
- ■ ¿Y luego podemos …?
- ● Vale. A las …
- ■ Después vamos a …
- ● Muy bien.

 De acuerdo.

 No tengo ganas.

¡Ni en sueños!

Vale.

 6 Escucha y lee los textos. ¿Verdadero o falso? Escribe V o F.

Ejemplo: **1** V

1 Iker va a tomar el tren minero.
2 Conchita y Polita van a practicar las artes circenses.
3 Conchita y Polita no van a navegar por los rápidos del Río Rojo.
4 Iker va a explorar el mundo perdido del Jurásico y después va a practicar las artes circenses.
5 Conchita y Polita no se van a montar en la montaña rusa.
6 Iker se va a montar en la montaña rusa después del mundo perdido.

Iker

Primero voy a tomar el tren minero. Luego voy a navegar por los rápidos del Río Rojo. Después voy a explorar el mundo perdido del Jurásico y más tarde me voy a montar en la montaña rusa.

Me chiflan los parques de atracciones. Va a ser muy divertido pero no voy a practicar las artes circenses porque ¡no me gusta nada eso!

Primero vamos a practicar las artes circenses, ¡qué interesante! Luego vamos a navegar por los rápidos del Río Rojo. Y después vamos a explorar el mundo perdido del Jurásico.

Pero no nos vamos a montar en la montaña rusa. No queremos. Tenemos miedo. Vamos a ir a la cafetería y vamos a comer algo.

Conchita y Polita

me chiflan = *I am crazy about*
tenemos miedo = *we are frightened*
algo = *something*

 7 ¿Qué vas a hacer en el parque de atracciones? Escribe un texto.

Ejemplo: Primero voy a tomar el tren minero …

escuchar 1 Escucha y lee.

1

D > ¡Hola! Patricia. ¿Qué tal?
P > Bien, gracias, Diego.
¿Y tú? ¿Cómo estás?

2

D > Muy bien, gracias. 😊
Dime Patricia, ¿te
gustaría salir conmigo?
P > ¿Adónde?

3

D > Pues, no sé.
Podemos ir a la
bolera o quizás
a la playa. Tú
decides.

4

P > Me gustaría mucho ir a la
playa. Tomo el sol todos
los fines de semana.

5

viernes

P > ¿Cuándo nos vemos entonces?
D > ¿El viernes por la tarde?
P > No, Diego. Lo siento, el
viernes por la tarde no
puedo. Tengo que jugar al
fútbol. 😞

6

sábado

D > ¿El sábado por la tarde
entonces? ¿Está bien?
P > De acuerdo. Quedamos delante
de la estación.
D > Muy bien. ¡Hasta luego! 😊

conmigo = *with me*
quizás = *perhaps*
entonces = *then*

2 Con tu compañero/a, lee en voz alta la historia de Diego y Patricia.

 3 Contesta a las preguntas en español. ¡Cuidado con los verbos!

Ejemplo: **1** Diego quiere ir a la bolera o a la playa.

1 ¿Adónde quiere ir Diego?
2 ¿Adónde quiere ir Patricia?
3 ¿Qué hace Patricia el viernes por la tarde?
4 ¿Dónde van a quedar Diego y Patricia?

 4 Escucha y escribe el verbo correcto.

Ejemplo: **1** quieres

1 quiero / quieres
2 no quiere / no quiero
3 quieres / quiere
4 pueden / podemos
5 puede / puedes
6 puedo / no puedo

 5 Anita, Miriam, Juan y José quieren salir juntos. ¿Adónde van a ir? Escribe la letra correcta.
Anita, Miriam, Juan and José want to go out together. Where will they go? Write the correct letter.

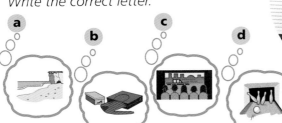

a   **b**   **c**   **d**

Juan   Anita   José   Miriam

Miriam quiere jugar a los bolos. No quiere ir al cine. No le gustan nada las películas.

Juan quiere ir al cine. No quiere ir de compras. Odia el centro comercial.

José quiere ir a la playa. Quiere escuchar música, mandar mensajes y leer.

Anita quiere ir de compras. Le gusta mucho ir al centro comercial. Odia la bolera.

 6 Escribe estas frases en español.

Ejemplo: **1** Quiero ir de compras este fin de semana.

1 I want to go shopping this weekend.
2 I have to go to the beach.
3 Vanesa wants to go to the cinema later.
4 Lola doesn't want to go to see the football match.
5 Pepe can't play football on Friday.
6 Norberto can do his homework tomorrow.

Palabras

¿Adónde vas?	*Where are you going (to)?*	**Este fin de semana**	*This weekend*
		(No) Voy a …	*I'm (not) going …*
Voy …	*I'm going …*	Vamos a …	*We're going …*
al centro comercial	*to the shopping centre*	escuchar música	*to listen to music*
al cine	*to the cinema*	ir al balneario	*to go to the spa*
al estadio	*to the stadium*	ir al casino	*to go to the casino*
al parque	*to the park*	ir a la peluquería	*to go to the hairdresser's*
al salón recreativo	*to the amusement arcade*		
		salir	*to go out*
a la bolera	*to the bowling alley*	ver la televisión	*to watch television*
a la discoteca	*to the disco*		
a la playa	*to the beach*	**¿Te gustaría salir?**	*Would you like to go out?*
¿Qué vas a hacer?	*What are you going to do?*	¿Te gustaría …?	*Would you like …?*
		ir al parque	*to go to the park*
Voy a …	*I'm going …*	ir a la bolera	*to go to the bowling alley*
bailar	*to dance/go dancing*		
ir de compras	*to go shopping*	ir de compras	*to go shopping*
jugar al fútbol	*to play football*		
jugar al futbolín	*to play table football*	**¿A qué hora?**	*At what time?*
jugar a los bolos	*to go bowling*	a la una	*at one o'clock*
tomar el sol	*to sunbathe*	a las tres	*at three o'clock*
ver un partido de fútbol	*to see a football match*	a las cinco y cuarto	*at quarter past five*
ver una película	*to see a film*	a las seis y media	*at half past six*
		a las siete menos cuarto	*at quarter to seven*
Mi semana	*My week*	a las ocho	*at eight o'clock*
el lunes	*Monday*	a las nueve	*at nine o'clock*
el martes	*Tuesday*		
el miércoles	*Wednesday*	**¿Dónde quedamos?**	*Where shall we meet?*
el jueves	*Thursday*	delante de la discoteca	*in front of the disco*
el viernes	*Friday*	detrás del centro comercial	*behind the shopping centre*
el sábado	*Saturday*	en el parque	*in the park*
el domingo	*Sunday*	en la bolera	*in the bowling alley*
		en la calle	*in the street*
¿Qué vas a hacer hoy?	*What are you going to do today?*	en tu casa	*at your house*
esta mañana	*this morning*	De acuerdo.	*OK.*
esta tarde	*this evening*	Vale.	*OK.*
esta noche	*tonight*	Muy bien.	*Fine.*
primero	*first*	No tengo ganas.	*I don't feel like it.*
luego	*then*	¡Ni hablar!	*No way!*
después	*afterwards*	¡Ni en sueños!	*In your dreams!*
más tarde	*later*	Bueno …	*Well …*
por último	*finally*	Pues …	*Well …*

A ver …	*Let's see …*	… y las soluciones	*… and solutions*
Hasta luego.	*See you later.*	Estoy de acuerdo con tu padre.	*I agree with your father.*
Adiós.	*Goodbye.*	Eres demasiado joven para ir a la discoteca.	*You're too young to go to the disco.*
Hasta pronto.	*See you soon.*	Tienes que …	*You must …*
		pensar en tu hermano	*think of your brother*
¿Quieres salir?	*Do you want to go out?*	presentar el amigo a tu madre	*introduce your friend to your mother*
¿Quieres …?	*Do you want …?*	salir más	*go out more*
chatear por internet	*to chat online*		
ir a la discoteca	*to go to the disco*	Palabras muy útiles	*Very useful words*
ir de compras	*to go shopping*	primero	*first*
jugar a los bolos	*to go bowling*	después	*afterwards*
jugar al fútbol	*to play football*	luego	*then*
salir	*to go out*	a (al)	*to (to the)*
ver un partido de fútbol	*to watch a football match*	delante de	*in front of*
ver una película	*to watch a film*	detrás de	*behind*
		para	*for, (in order) to*
Lo siento, no puedo.	*I'm sorry, I can't.*	¿dónde?	*where?*
No puedo salir.	*I can't go out.*	mi, tu, su (mis, tus, sus)	*my, your, his/her*
¿Por qué?	*Why?*		
Porque …	*Because …*		
no quiero	*I don't want to*		
no tengo dinero	*I don't have any money*		
no tengo tiempo	*I don't have any time*		
Tengo que …	*I have to …*		
hacer mis deberes	*do my homework*		
lavarme el pelo	*wash my hair*		
ordenar mi dormitorio	*tidy my room*		
pasear al perro	*walk the dog*		

Los problemas …   *Problems …*

Tengo un problema.	*I have a problem.*
¿Qué voy a hacer?	*What am I going to do?*
Mis padres dicen que …	*My parents say …*
¡No es justo!	*It's not fair!*
Soy demasiado joven.	*I'm too young.*
¿Qué le puedo decir a mi madre?	*What can I say to my mother?*

Estrategia

Looking up new words

Dictionaries can tell you a lot about new words. Most of them use these abbreviations: *nm, nf, adj, vt, prep*. For example, *nm* tells you a word is a masculine noun; *vt* tells you it's a verb. What do you think the others tell you?

Look up the words below in a dictionary. (They are all used on page 33.) Note down what each word means and what sort of word it is. For example: **joven** = *young* (adjective).

joven	tiempo	vida	triste
decir	pensar		

I ¿Adónde fuiste?

- Saying where you went on hol.
- Saying what it was like

escuchar 1 Escucha y lee. (1–16)

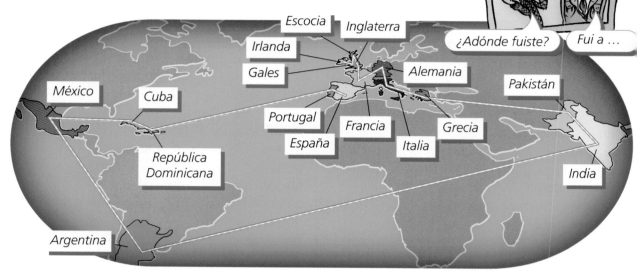

Escocia
Inglaterra
Irlanda
Gales
Alemania
Pakistán
México
Cuba
Portugal
Francia
Grecia
España
Italia
República Dominicana
India
Argentina

¿Adónde fuiste?
Fui a …

hablar 2 Con tu compañero/a, lee estas frases. ¿Qué significan?
Read these phrases with your partner. What do they mean?

fui = *I went*
fue = *it was*

¿Cómo fue?

Fue …

estupendo
genial
guay
aburrido
horrible
un desastre

Check you know the meanings of these words.
Which strategies did you use?
- I thought of a similar English word.
- I used the pictures as clues.
- I used a dictionary.
- I used the *Vocabulario*.

escuchar 3 Escucha y escribe el país y la opinión. (1–5)

Ejemplo: **1** México – genial

Pay special attention to these sounds:

x   'ks': ex**ó**tico
           'ch' in 'loch': Mé**x**ico
g + **e** or **i**   'ch' in 'loch': Ar**g**entina, **g**enial
c + **e** or **i**   'th': Fran**c**ia, Gre**c**ia, Esco**c**ia

Listen and repeat these phrases with a partner.

Mé**x**ico es ex**ó**tico.
Ar**g**entina es **g**enial.
Esco**c**ia es pre**c**iosa.

4 Escucha y lee.

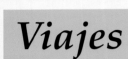

www.guia-del-viajero.com

Viajes

- Opiniones ▶
- Destinos famosos ▶
- Rutas por España ▶
- Recomendamos ▶

Javier
El año pasado fui a Francia de vacaciones. Fui con mis padres. A mi madre le encanta ir de compras y visitar monumentos pero a mí no me gusta nada. Fue aburrido. Lo siento, pero no me gusta Francia. **Leer**

Antonio
El año pasado fui a Cuba de vacaciones. Fui con mis padres y fue guay. Me gusta mucho bailar y me encanta el 'son', la música cubana. También me gusta tomar el sol y en Cuba hace buen tiempo. **Leer**

Jessica
El año pasado fui a República Dominicana de vacaciones con mis amigos. Fui a la playa todos los días y luego por la tarde fui a la discoteca. Jugué al béisbol, un deporte muy popular allí. Fue genial. **Leer**

béisbol = *baseball*
allí = *there*

¿Con quién fuiste?

Fui …   con mi familia   con mis padres   con mis amigos

---

5 Lee los textos otra vez.
Copia y rellena la tabla en inglés.

Name	Destination	Opinion	Extra details
Javier			

6 Con tu compañero/a, haz diálogos con las personas del ejercicio 4.

- ● ¿Adónde fuiste de vacaciones, <u>Javier</u>?
- ■ Fui a <u>Francia</u>.
- ● ¿Con quién fuiste?
- ■ Fui con <u>mis padres</u>.
- ● ¿Cómo fue?
- ■ Fue <u>aburrido</u>.

 7 Escribe un texto para la página web.

1 **Escucha y escribe la ciudad y el medio de transporte. (1–8)**
Listen and note down the city and the means of transport.

Ejemplo: **1** Madrid – coach

¿Adónde fuiste de vacaciones?

Fui a …

¿Cómo fuis...

en autocar

Los viajes de Víctor Viaje

en monopatín

en avión

en bicicleta

en tren

Pamplona

Santiago de Compostela

Madrid

Toledo

Palma de Mallorca

Valencia

Córdoba

Granada

Lanjarón

en barco

en coche

a pie

2 **Con tu compañero/a, haz diálogos utilizando los dibujos del ejercicio 1.**

- ¿Adónde fuiste de vacaciones?
- Fui a <u>Madrid</u>.
- ¿Cómo fuiste?
- Fui <u>en autocar</u>.

3 **Describe el viaje de Víctor Viaje (ejercicio 1).**

Ejemplo: Fui a Madrid en autocar, fui a …

4 Escucha. Copia y rellena la tabla. (1–4)

	¿Cuándo?	¿Dónde?	¿Cómo?	¿Con quién?	¿Cómo fue?
1	el verano pasado	Madrid	tren	amigos	guay

El año pasado …
El invierno pasado …
El verano pasado …

Jessica e Isabel, su abuela. Dos aventuras distintas.

5 Lee los textos. Escribe los medios de transporte.

Ejemplo: Jessica – plane, …   Isabel – boat, …

---
miespacio.com

Vídeos | Favoritos | Foros | Grupos | Música

Mis vacaciones en 2007 – Jessica

El año pasado fui a Palma de Mallorca de vacaciones y fue genial. Fui con mi mejor amiga, Alicia, en avión. Palma, la capital, está en la costa. Es una ciudad importante.

Fuimos a la playa a pie todos los días. Por las tardes fuimos de compras, ¡me encanta comprar ropa! Por las noches fuimos a la discoteca en monopatín.

---

sur = south

16 de septiembre de 1957

Las aventuras de Isabel Gómez

Mi viaje a Perú fue estupendo. Fui a Lima en barco. De Lima fui a Tacna, en el sur de Perú, en autocar.

Luego fui a Arequipa, primero en bicicleta y después a caballo. Me encanta montar a caballo.

De Arequipa fui a Cuzco en tren y fue genial. Cuzco es la capital del Imperio Inca.

Luego fui al santuario de Machu Picchu a pie. Está en unas montañas muy altas. Es tranquilo y precioso.

6 Lee los textos otra vez. Corrige cada frase.

Ejemplo: **1** Jessica fue a Mallorca con su amiga.

1 Jessica fue a Mallorca con su hermano.
2 Su mejor amiga se llama Louise.
3 Por la noche fueron al teatro.
4 Palma está en las montañas.
5 Isabel fue a Lima en avión.
6 Tacna está en el norte de Perú.
7 Cuzco es la capital de los Aztecas.
8 Machu Picchu es feo y aburrido.

Gramática

The preterite (simple past tense)

The preterite of **ir** *(to go)* and **ser** *(to be)* is the same! Learn it by heart.

fui	I went	I was
fuiste	you went	you were
fue	he/she went	he/she was
fuimos	we went	we were
fuisteis	you (pl.) went	you (pl.) were
fueron	they went	they were

Para saber más   página 132; ej. 12

- Saying what you did on holiday
- Using the preterite of **-ar** verbs

escuchar
1 Escucha y escribe la letra correcta. (1–10)

¿Qué hiciste?

Ejemplo: **1** j

a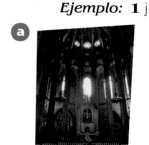
Visité monumentos.

b
Bailé.

c
Monté en bicicleta.

d
Descansé.

e
Mandé mensajes.

f
Escuché música.

g
Tomé el sol.

h
Saqué fotos.

i
Jugué al voleibol en la playa.

j
Fui de excursión.

Gramática

The preterite of *-ar* verbs

visitar   *to visit*

visit**é**	*I visited*
visit**aste**	*you visited*
visit**ó**	*he/she visited*
visit**amos**	*we visited*
visit**asteis**	*you (plural) visited*
visit**aron**	*they visited*

Practise saying these, with the stress on the accented letter:

visit**é**, bail**é**, mont**é**, tom**é**, mand**é**, escuch**é**

Para saber más   página 132; ej. 10

hablar
2 Con tu compañero/a, haz diálogos.

- ¿Qué hiciste?
- Tomé el sol y también visité monumentos.

1

2

3

4

5

Escucha a Raúl y haz una lista en inglés de las actividades. (8 actividades)

Ejemplo: relaxed, …

Pon el texto en un orden lógico. Escucha y comprueba tus respuestas.

primero	*first*
después	*afterwards*
luego	*then*

Ejemplo: 7, …

1 Tomé el sol en la playa y jugué al voleibol también. Descansé, escuché música y mandé mensajes a mis amigos. Fue estupendo. Por la noche bailé en la discoteca con mi hermana y fue genial.

2 Un día fuimos de excursión en Trieste. Primero visité monumentos y saqué fotos. Luego fuimos a un restaurante italiano. Fue genial.

3 Vivo en Granada, en el sur de España.

4 Está en el norte de Italia, en la costa.

5 El año pasado fui de vacaciones a Italia con mi familia. Fui a Trieste.

6 Fuimos en avión. Fue guay.

7 Me llamo Chema. Soy español y tengo catorce años.

- **g + e/i → gu**
  ju**g**ar → ju**gu**é
  Ju**gu**é al voleibol. *I played volleyball.*
- **c + e/i → qu**
  sa**c**ar → sa**qu**é
  Sa**qu**é fotos. *I took photos.*

The silent **u** keeps the pronunciation the same.

Escucha otra vez. ¿Qué actividades menciona Chema? Escribe las letras del ejercicio 1. (9 actividades)

Empareja las preguntas con el texto del ejercicio 4.

Ejemplo: **a** 3

a ¿Dónde vives?
b ¿Adónde fuiste de vacaciones?
c ¿Dónde está?
d ¿Cómo fuiste y cómo fue?

e ¿Qué hiciste?
f Describe un día.
g ¿Cómo te llamas? ¿Cuál es tu nacionalidad?

7 Describe tus vacaciones.
Use Chema's text and the questions in exercise 6 to help you.

Mini-test

I can
- say where I went on holiday
- say what it was like
- say what I did on holiday
- **G** use the preterite of **ser** and **ir**
- **G** use the preterite of regular **-ar** verbs

4 ¿Qué tal lo pasaste?

- Giving more details of your holidays
- Expressing opinions about past events

escuchar 1 Escucha y repite.

¿Qué tal lo pasaste?

¡Lo pasé bomba!

Lo pasé fenomenal.

Lo pasé guay.

Lo pasé bien.

Lo pasé mal.

¿Qué tal lo pasaste? *What sort of a time did you have?*
Lo pasé bomba. *I had a fantastic time.*

Sometimes things don't translate directly word for word.
Learn phrases like these by heart.

---

escuchar 2 Escucha y contesta a las preguntas para cada persona. (1–5)

- *Where did they go?*
- *When?*
- *How long for?*
- *How was it?*

¿Cuándo?	El año pasado
	El invierno pasado
	El verano pasado
¿Cuánto tiempo?	Diez días
	Una semana
	Dos semanas
	Un mes

escribir 3 Separa las palabras y escribe las preguntas y respuestas.

¿adóndefuiste?fuiacuba¿cuándo?elañopasado¿cuántotiempo?dossemanas¿quétallopasaste?lopaséfenomenal

4 Con tu compañero/a, haz diálogos.

- ¿Adónde fuiste?
- ■ Fui a <u>México</u>.
- ¿Cómo fuiste?
- ■ Fui <u>en avión</u>.
- ¿Cuánto tiempo pasaste allí?
- ■ Pasé <u>dos semanas</u>.
- ¿Con quién fuiste?
- ■ Fui <u>con mi familia</u>.
- ¿Qué hiciste?
- ■ <u>Fui de excursión y visité monumentos.</u>
- ¿Qué tal lo pasaste?
- ■ <u>¡Lo pasé guay!</u>

México

guay

Grecia

bien

Irlanda

bomba

5 Escribe un diálogo del ejercicio 4.

6 Escucha y canta.

7 Busca estas frases en español en la canción.

Ejemplo: **1** ¿Adónde fuiste?

1 Where did you go?
2 How did you travel?
3 What did you do?
4 How was it?
5 tell me
6 with
7 I went
8 I played

Mis vacaciones

Fui de vacaciones
¡la playa es genial!
Fui de vacaciones
¡la playa es genial!
¿Qué tal lo pasaste?
¡Lo pasé fenomenal!

¿Adónde fuiste?
Fui a la playa de Gijón.
¿Cómo fuiste?
Fui en barco y en avión.

¿Con quién fuiste?
Con mi hermana Marisol.
Dime, ¿qué hiciste?
Jugué al fútbol y al voleibol.

Fui de vacaciones …

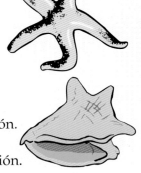

1 Escucha y lee. Luego empareja los textos con las fotos correctas. (1–3)

www.vacaciones-inolvidables.es

Vacaciones divinas

Paco Generalmente **voy** de vacaciones a República Dominicana con mis amigos en avión. Por la tarde **juego** al fútbol en la playa. **Salgo** con mis amigos por la noche, **vamos** a la cafetería, a la discoteca, y al salón recreativo también.

El verano pasado **fui** a Portugal con mis amigos. **Fui** en tren y en autocar, **fue** guay. **Pinté** mucho, ¡**me encanta** pintar! y **escuché** música. **Descansé** y lo **pasé** bien.

Natalia Normalmente **voy** a Milán con mi familia en coche. **Voy** de compras, **voy** a la peluquería y a la sauna. **Mando** mensajes a mis amigos todos los días.

El año pasado **fui** a Cuba con mi hermano. **Fuimos** en avión. **Monté** en bicicleta y **bailé** salsa. **Hice** excursiones muy interesantes. **Jugué** al fútbol en la playa. Lo **pasé** fenomenal.

James Normalmente no **voy** de vacaciones. **Me quedo** en casa. **Juego** con el ordenador, **chateo** por internet o a veces **mando** mensajes. **Hago** mis deberes y **estudio** mucho también.

Pero el año pasado **fui** a la playa en España, y lo **pasé** bomba. ¡**Fue** genial! **Descansé**, **hice** yoga y **tomé** el sol. **Fui** con mi hermano Rod. **Fuimos** en avión.

pinté = *I painted*

1

2

3

2 Escribe los datos sobre Paco, Natalia y James en inglés.

	Name	Normally	Last year
1		goes to Dominican Republic ...	

Gramática

Present or past? Look for:

	Present	Past
time expressions	normalmente generalmente	el año pasado el verano pasado
verbs	voy, juego, tomo, monto, descanso, mando, pinto	fui, jugué, tomé, monté, descansé, mandé, pinté
verbs in questions	¿Adónde vas? ¿Qué haces?	¿Adónde fuiste? ¿Qué hiciste?

Para saber más   página 133; ej. 14

leer 3 Lee los textos otra vez. ¿Quién es?

Who …
1 likes going out at night?
2 normally comes back from holiday with a different hairstyle?
3 took two different forms of transport to their holiday destination last year?
4 likes to spend time with friends?
5 rested in the sun on a holiday last year?
6 normally spends a lot of time at home?
7 did a lot of physical activity on holiday?
8 is a good student at school?
9 took up painting on their recent holiday?

hablar 4 Con tu compañero/a, pregunta y contesta por Paco, Natalia y James.

1 ¿Adónde vas de vacaciones generalmente?
2 ¿Adónde fuiste de vacaciones el año pasado?
3 ¿Cómo vas normalmente?
4 ¿Cómo fuiste?
5 ¿Con quién vas de vacaciones?
6 ¿Con quién fuiste?
7 ¿Qué haces normalmente?
8 ¿Qué hiciste?

escuchar 5 Escucha y escribe los datos de las vacaciones en inglés. (1–3)

	Normally …	Last year …
1	England, excursions …	

escuchar 6 Escucha otra vez y escribe los verbos que entiendes. (1–3)

	Present	Preterite
1	vas, …	fuiste, …

hablar 7 Haz una presentación sobre tus vacaciones ideales. Utiliza las preguntas del ejercicio 4.

Resumen

Unidad 1

I can
- ask someone where they went on holiday ¿Adónde fuiste?
- say where I went on holiday Fui a Portugal, España, Cuba, Grecia, …
- say what it was like Fue guay. Fue genial. Fue aburrido.
- say who I travelled with Fui con mi familia. Fui con mis padres.

Unidad 2

I can
- ask someone how they travelled ¿Cómo fuiste?
- say how I travelled Fui en avión, en coche, en barco, a pie …
- use expressions referring to the past el año pasado, el invierno pasado, el verano pasado
- **G** use the preterite of **ser** and **ir** **Fui** en autocar. **Fue** fatal.
  Fuimos en coche. **Fue** genial.

Unidad 3

I can
- ask someone what they did on holiday ¿Qué hiciste?
- say what I did on holiday Visité monumentos. Monté en bicicleta.
  Tomé el sol.
- use sequencing words **Primero** visité monumentos y saqué fotos.
  Luego fuimos a un restaurante italiano.
- **G** understand the preterite of **-ar** verbs visité, visitaste, visitó

Unidad 4

I can
- ask someone if they had a good time ¿Qué tal lo pasaste?
- say whether I had a good time ¡Lo pasé bomba!
  Lo pasé bien. Lo pasé mal.
- say how long I went on holiday for Pasé dos semanas.
- **G** use question words ¿Con quién fuiste? ¿Cuándo?
  ¿Cuánto tiempo pasaste allí?

Unidad 5

I can
- **G** use the present and the preterite together Normalmente **voy** a Nueva York y **voy** de compras.
  El año pasado **fui** a Cuba con mi hermano.
  Fuimos en avión y en coche.
- **G** recognise whether a question is in the past or present tense ¿Adónde vas? ¿Adónde fuiste?
- **G** use time expressions referring to the past and present el año pasado, generalmente, normalmente

1 Escucha. Copia y rellena la tabla. (1–5)

	País	Transporte	Opinión
1	Francia	coche	horrible

 2 Con tu compañero/a, pregunta y contesta.

● ¿Qué hiciste?
■ 'e': Mandé mensajes.

 3 Lee el texto. Contesta a las preguntas en inglés.

Jorge

Normalmente voy a Francia de vacaciones con mi familia, pero el verano pasado fui a Italia con mis amigos. Fuimos en tren. Fue genial.

Fuimos a Nápoles. Está en el sur de Italia en la costa. ¡Lo pasé bomba!

Visité monumentos y fui de excursión. Bailé y escuché música también. Fue guay.

Nápoles

1 Where does Jorge normally spend his holidays?
2 When did he go to Italy?
3 How did Jorge travel?
4 Where exactly is Naples?
5 What did he do?
6 How was his holiday?

 4 Separa estas preguntas. Luego escribe las respuestas utilizando los dibujos.

 ¿adóndefuistecómofuisteconquiénfuistequéhicistequétallopasaste?

bomba

Lee los textos. Escucha y pon las frases en el orden correcto.

Ejemplo: c, …

En 1492 hizo su primer viaje. Primero fue a San Salvador y luego a Cuba.

Regresó del Nuevo Mundo con el cacao, la patata y el maíz.

Cristóbal Colón fue explorador.

Encontró para España una ruta desde Europa hasta América – un nuevo continente.

Después fue a La Española, otra isla en el mar Caribe.

 Busca estas frases en español en el texto.

Ejemplo: **1** Primero fue a San Salvador.

1 First he went to San Salvador.
2 He came back from the New World.
3 Christopher Columbus was an explorer.
4 Afterwards he went to La Española.
5 He found, for Spain, a route from Europe to America.

 Lee las frases. Tu compañero/a dice 'sí' o 'no'.

Ejemplo: **1** No, no es una isla en el mar Mediterráneo. Es una isla en el mar Caribe.

1 La Española es una isla en el mar Mediterráneo.
2 Cristóbal Colón regresó del Nuevo Mundo con el cacao, la patata y el maíz.
3 El primer viaje de Cristóbal Colón fue a San Salvador y luego a Cuba.
4 Cristóbal Colón fue profesor.
5 Cristóbal Colón encontró para Inglaterra una ruta desde Europa hasta América.

4 Copia y completa el texto con las palabras del cuadro.

Ejemplo: … (**1**) fui de viaje …

San Salvador

Cuba

La Española

Me llamo Roberto Buitrago y (1) _____ de viaje con el famoso Cristóbal Colón en 1492. Primero (2) _____ a San Salvador. Probé el cacao. (3) _____ delicioso. Muy, muy bueno. Luego (4) _____ en nuestro barco a Cuba. (5) _____ genial. Después, fuimos a La Española, otra isla en el mar Caribe. (6) _____ estupendo. No quiero regresar. ¡Me quedo aquí!

fui   fue   fue   fue   fuimos   fuimos

5 Contesta a las preguntas en inglés.

1 What was Roberto Buitrago's connection with Christopher Columbus?
2 What did he do on San Salvador? What did he think of it?
3 Describe the journey to Cuba.
4 Where did they go after Cuba?
5 What were Roberto's impressions of the places they saw?

6 Lee el texto. Busca las palabras que no entiendes en el Vocabulario.

> Make a list of all the cognates in the text. Tell your partner how you worked out their meaning.

www.miparaiso.com

Parque Nacional Tortuguero – Costa Rica

El Parque Nacional Tortuguero está en la costa caribeña, en el norte de Costa Rica. El parque es importante porque la tortuga verde viene a desovar en la playa.

Hay muchas lagunas y canales en el parque. Son el hábitat para cocodrilos, manatíes, cangrejos y para cincuenta y dos especies de peces.

El parque fue creado para proteger la flora y la fauna de la región. Hay jaguares, ranas venenosas, monos y arañas. También hay muchas especies de pájaros.

El parque es una reserva natural muy importante. Es el mejor ejemplo de un bosque tropical húmedo del mundo.

escuchar 1 Escucha y lee.

1

P – Diego, ¿adónde fuiste de vacaciones el año pasado?
D – Pues, no fui de vacaciones, me quedé en Barcelona, pero hice excursiones …

2

P – ¿Ah, sí? ¿Adónde fuiste?
D – Fui a Cadaqués en barco con un amigo.

3

P – ¿Dónde está?
D – ¿¡Dónde está Cadaqués!? Ah sí, eres mexicana … A ver, Cadaqués está al norte de Barcelona.

4

D – Es un pueblo muy famoso de pescadores y artistas.
P – ¿Y qué hiciste en Cadaqués?

5

D – Tomé el sol, jugué al fútbol en la playa y visité la casa de Salvador Dalí. Es un pintor surrealista muy famoso.
P – ¿Dalí? Ah sí, me gustan mucho sus pinturas. Es mi pintor favorito.

6

P – ¿Te gusta el dibujo, Diego?
D – Sí, me encanta el dibujo.
P – A mí también me encanta el dibujo …

hablar 2 Con tu compañero/a, lee en voz alta la historia de Diego y Patricia.

3 Con tu compañero/a, pregunta y contesta.

1 ¿Qué hizo Diego el año pasado durante las vacaciones?
2 ¿Cómo fue a Cadaqués?
3 ¿Con quién?
4 ¿Dónde está Cadaqués?
5 ¿Qué hizo Diego en Cadaqués?
6 ¿Qué le gusta a Diego?

4 Copia y completa el texto.

Ejemplo: … fue a Cadaqués en (**1**) barco …

El año pasado Diego fue a Cadaqués en ⁽¹⁾  con un amigo.

Cadaqués está al ⁽²⁾ de Barcelona. Es un ⁽³⁾ muy famoso

de pescadores y artistas. Diego tomó el ⁽⁴⁾, jugó al ⁽⁵⁾ en la

y visitó la casa de Salvador Dalí.

5 Escucha y lee el texto sobre Dalí. Luego copia y rellena la tabla.

ser   estudiar   ir   utilizar   trabajar   regresar

Infinitive	English	Preterite	English
ser	to be	fue	he was

ZONA CULTURA

Dalí

Salvador Dalí (1904–89) fue pintor. Estudió en Madrid. Utilizó imágenes surrealistas en sus dibujos.

En 1940 fue a los Estados Unidos. Luego en 1948 regresó a España. Trabajó en Cadaqués hasta su muerte.

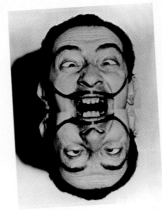

su muerte = *his death*

6 Elige a una persona histórica famosa y describe su vida.
Utiliza el texto sobre Dalí como modelo.

Palabras

¿Adónde fuiste? — *Where did you go (to)?*

el año pasado	last year
Fui a …	I went to …
Alemania	Germany
Argentina	Argentina
Cuba	Cuba
Escocia	Scotland
España	Spain
Francia	France
Gales	Wales
Grecia	Greece
India	India
Inglaterra	England
Irlanda	Ireland
Italia	Italy
México	Mexico
Pakistán	Pakistan
Portugal	Portugal
República Dominicana	the Dominican Republic

¿Cómo fue? — *What was it like?*

Fue …	It was …
estupendo	fantastic
genial	brilliant
guay	great, cool
aburrido	boring
horrible	awful
un desastre	a disaster

¿Con quién fuiste? — *Who did you go with?*

Fui …	I went …
con mi familia	with my family
con mis padres	with my parents
con mis amigos	with my friends

¡Buen viaje! — *Have a good trip!*

¿Adónde fuiste de vacaciones?	Where did you go (to) on holiday?
Fui a Madrid.	I went to Madrid.
¿Cómo fuiste?	How did you go?
Fui …	I went …
a pie	on foot
en autocar	by bus
en avión	by plane
en barco	by boat
en bicicleta	by bike
en coche	by car
en monopatín	by skateboard
en tren	by train
El invierno pasado …	Last winter …
El verano pasado …	Last summer …

¿Qué hiciste? — *What did you do?*

Bailé.	I danced.
Descansé.	I had a rest/break.
Escuché música.	I listened to music.
Fui de excursión.	I went on an outing.
Jugué al voleibol en la playa.	I played volleyball on the beach.
Mandé mensajes.	I sent messages.
Monté en bicicleta.	I rode my bike.
Saqué fotos.	I took photos.
Tomé el sol.	I sunbathed.
Visité monumentos.	I visited monuments.

¿Qué tal lo pasaste? — *What sort of time did you have?*

¡Lo pasé bomba!	I had a fantastic time!
¡Lo pasé fenomenal!	I had a wonderful time!
¡Lo pasé guay!	I had a great time!
¡Lo pasé bien!	I had a good time!
¡Lo pasé mal!	I had a bad time!

¿Cuánto tiempo pasaste allí?	How much time did you spend there?
Pasé …	I spent …
diez días	ten days
una semana	a week
dos semanas	two weeks
un mes	a month

Mis vacaciones	**My holidays**
Generalmente …	Usually …
Normalmente …	Normally …
me quedo en casa	I stay at home
salgo con mis amigos por la noche	I go out at night with friends
vamos a la cafetería	we go to the café
voy a España	I go to Spain

Pero el año pasado …	But last year …
fui a Cuba	I went to Cuba
fuimos en avión	we went by plane
fuimos a un restaurante italiano	we went to an Italian restaurant
hice excursiones muy interesantes	I went on very interesting outings
jugué al fútbol	I played football
pinté	I painted

Palabras muy útiles	**Very useful words**
a	to
con	with
en	in, by
¿cómo?	how?, what … like?
¿adónde?	(to) where?
¿quién?	who?, whom?
¿qué?	what?

Estrategia

Mnemonics

A mnemonic helps you to remember a difficult word or expression. A common type of mnemonic is a made-up phrase consisting of words whose first letters spell the word you want to remember. For example, to remind you how to spell **Inglaterra**, you could try using this mnemonic:

I
Never
Get
Long
At
Teatime
Eating
Ripe
Red
Apples

● Choose a word from Module 3 that you want to learn to spell and make up a mnemonic for it.

1 ¿Qué desayunas?

escuchar 1 Escucha y escribe la letra o las letras correctas. (1–13)

Ejemplo: **1** b

¿Qué desayunas? ⟩ Desayuno …

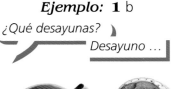

a cereales **b** tostadas

c magdalenas

¿Qué comes? ⟩ Como …

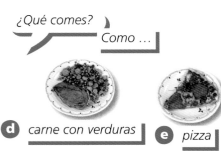

d carne con verduras **e** pizza

f patatas fritas

¿Qué meriendas? ⟩ Meriendo …

g galletas **h** fruta

i un bocadillo

¿Qué cenas? ⟩ Ceno …

j pescado con ensalada **k** pasta **l** pollo

¿Qué bebes? ⟩ Bebo …

m Cola Cao **n** té **o** zumo de naranja **p** nada

There are different verbs in Spanish for talking about different meals.

desayunar	*to eat breakfast*	Desayuno cereales.	*I eat cereals for breakfast.*
comer	*to eat lunch*	Como pizza.	*I eat pizza for lunch.*
merendar	*to eat tea*	Meriendo galletas.	*I eat biscuits for tea.*
cenar	*to eat dinner*	Ceno pollo.	*I eat chicken for dinner.*

---

hablar 2 Pregunta y contesta. Di la letra correcta del ejercicio 1.

● ¿Qué desayunas?
■ Desayuno tostadas.
● b

¿Qué desayunas?   ¿Qué meriendas?   ¿Qué bebes?

¿Qué comes?   ¿Qué cenas?

escuchar 3 Escucha a Sergio y contesta a las preguntas. Escribe las letras del ejercicio 1 o una hora.

Ejemplo: **1** a

1 ¿Qué desayuna Sergio?
2 ¿Qué bebe?
3 ¿A qué hora desayuna?
4 ¿Qué come?
5 ¿A qué hora come?
6 ¿Qué merienda?
7 ¿A qué hora cena?
8 ¿Qué cena?

¿A qué hora cenas?
At what time do you have dinner?
¿Qué cenas?
What do you have for dinner?

4 Escucha otra vez. ¿Qué palabras del cuadro entiendes? ¿Qué significan?

Ejemplo: normalmente = normally

siempre
normalmente
a veces
de vez en cuando
nunca

 5 Empareja las bandejas con los animales. (Sobra una bandeja.)
Match up the trays to the animals. (There is one tray too many.)

1 Normalmente no desayuno nada. A veces a mediodía como un bocadillo o una pizza. ¡Me gusta mucho la pizza!
Normalmente meriendo a las cinco con mis amigos los ratones. Meriendo galletas y fruta. ¿Y qué ceno? Normalmente ceno carne con verduras o pescado con ensalada.

2 Desayuno cereales y té. Siempre desayuno a las ocho. ¡El desayuno es una comida muy importante!
Como pescado. No meriendo y nunca ceno. Generalmente no tengo hambre, pero me gusta beber cócteles.

3 Tengo hambre todo el tiempo. Normalmente desayuno tostadas y zumo de naranja. Desayuno a las siete.
A veces a mediodía como un bocadillo con mi novia Adelina. Meriendo fruta, me gusta mucho. Generalmente ceno pollo. Normalmente ceno a las nueve.

Roberto el Ratón

Serafina la Serpiente

tengo hambre = *I'm hungry*
todo el tiempo = *all the time*
novia = *girlfriend*

Pepe el Perro

 6 Contesta al sondeo. Cambia los datos subrayados y completa las frases.

1	¿A qué hora desayunas?	Desayuno a las siete o a las ...
2	¿Qué desayunas?	A veces desayuno cereales. También desayuno ...
3	¿A qué hora comes?	Como a las dos o a las ...
4	¿Qué comes?	Como pollo. Nunca como ...
5	¿A qué hora meriendas?	Meriendo a las cinco.
6	¿Qué meriendas?	De vez en cuando meriendo galletas.
7	¿A qué hora cenas?	Normalmente ceno a las nueve.
8	¿Qué cenas?	Ceno pescado. Nunca ceno ...

escuchar 1 Escucha y repite.

cien (100)
ciento diez (110)
doscientos (200)
trescientos (300)
cuatrocientos (400)
quinientos (500)

seiscientos (600)
setecientos (700)
ochocientos (800)
novecientos (900)
mil (1000)

hablar 2 Juega con dos compañeros. Una persona dice un número del ejercicio 1. Hay que escribir el número correcto.

● novecientos
■ [escribe:] 900

escuchar 3 Escucha y escribe la letra correcta. (1–12)

¿Qué quieres?

…, por favor.

Ejemplo: **1** i

a
un kilo de peras

b
medio kilo de tomates

c
dos kilos de manzanas

d
un kilo de zanahorias

e
cien gramos de jamón

f
doscientos gramos de ques

g
quinientos gramos de uvas

h
un chorizo

i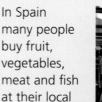
una lechuga

j
una barra de pan

k
una botella de agua

l
un cartón de leche

In Spain many people buy fruit, vegetables, meat and fish at their local market.

4 Escucha y escribe el precio correcto. (a–j)

Ejemplo: **a** 1,00€

1,50€   3,75€   1,00€   4,25€   3,50€

2,50€   0,80€   2,20€   2,25€   1,30€

> The currency used in Spain, and in most European countries, is the euro. There are 100 cents (**céntimos**) in one euro.

5 Con tu compañero/a, haz diálogos cambiando los datos subrayados.

● ¿Qué quieres?
■ <u>Un kilo de tomates</u>, por favor.
● ¿Algo más?
■ Sí, quiero … y … también.
● ¿Algo más?
■ Nada más, gracias. ¿Cuánto cuesta?
● <u>Dos</u> euros y <u>setenta y cinco</u> céntimos.

> ¿Algo más? = *Anything else?*
> Nada más. = *Nothing else.*

6 Escucha y canta.

Para mis amigos

Fui al mercado y compré …
Medio kilo de tomates para Pilates.

Fui al mercado y compré …
Una barra de pan para Sebastián

Fui al mercado y compré …
Cien gramos de jamón para Ramón,

Fui al mercado y compré …
Un pepino para Severino,

> pepino = *cucumber*

Fui al mercado y compré …
Una lechuga para mi tortuga,

Fui al mercado y compré …
Dos kilos de manzanas para mis hermanas,

Gramática

The preterite of *-ar* verbs

comprar	*to buy*
compr**é**	*I bought*
compr**aste**	*you bought*
compr**ó**	*he/she bought*
compr**amos**	*we bought*
compr**asteis**	*you (plural) bought*
compr**aron**	*they bought*

escuchar 1 Escucha y escribe el plato y la letra correcta. (1–12)

Ejemplo: **1** primer plato – b

¿Qué vas a tomar?

¿Qué va a tomar?

> What are you going to have?
>
> **tú** = *you (singular, familiar)* ¿Qué **vas** a tomar?
> **usted** = *you (singular, polite)* ¿Qué **va** a tomar?
>
> **Usted** is the polite 'you'. It uses the same verb form as 'he/she'.

El girasol Menú

De primer plato …

a una sopa
b unas gambas
c una ensalada

De postre …

g un flan
h un helado
i fruta

De segundo plato …

d pescado
e pollo
f una paella de mariscos

Para beber …

j agua
k una Coca-Cola
l una limonada

hablar 2 Con tu compañero/a, haz diálogos.

● ¿Qué vas a tomar?
■ De primer plato quiero …
■ De segundo plato quiero …
■ De postre quiero …
● ¿Para beber?
■ Quiero …

3 **Escucha y lee.**

Alicia	Tengo hambre. Quiero <u>un helado de chocolate</u>. ¿Qué vas a tomar?
Javier	No tengo hambre pero tengo sed. Quiero <u>una limonada</u>.
Camarero	¿Qué va a tomar?
Alicia	<u>Un helado de chocolate</u>, por favor.
Camarero	¿Y usted? ¿Qué va a tomar?
Javier	<u>Una limonada</u>, por favor.
Camarero	¿Algo más?
Javier	Nada más. La cuenta, por favor.

La cuenta, por favor. = *The bill, please.*

Some expressions just don't translate word for word!

Tengo hambre. | *I'm hungry.* | *Tengo sed.* | *I'm thirsty.*

 4 **Escucha y escribe las letras correctas del ejercicio 1. (1–3)**

Ejemplo: **1** g, k

 5 **Con otras dos personas, haz diálogos, cambiando los datos subrayados del ejercicio 3.**

❶    **❷**    **❸**

 6 **Escribe un diálogo del ejercicio 5.**

7 **Escucha y lee el texto 'El tapeo'. Escribe las letras de los dibujos mencionados.**

a   **b**   **c**   **d**   **e**   **f**   **g**   **h**

ZONA CULTURA

El tapeo

El tapeo es una costumbre muy famosa en España. El tapeo consiste en ir de bar en bar tomando tapas de jamón serrano, queso, tortilla o gambas, con vino o cerveza.

Mini-test

I can
- say what I have for breakfast, lunch, tea and dinner
- ask someone what they have for breakfast, lunch, tea and dinner
- say at what time I have different meals
- buy food in a market
- order in a restaurant
- **G** use the preterite to say what I bought

- Talking about a past meal
- Using the preterite of **-er** and **-ir** verbs

escuchar **1** Escucha y lee.

Mi cena con David

Alex Smith

El fin de semana pasado salí *con David Beckham.*
Fui *a Madrid en avión y* fui *a un restaurante muy
caro con David. ¡*Fue *guay! El restaurante se llama
El Mesón madrileño.*

De primer plato comí *una ensalada y David,
gambas. De segundo plato* compartimos *una
paella.*

De postre comí *un helado de chocolate
– ¡delicioso! – David no* comió *nada.* Bebimos
agua.

Durante la cena, David recibió *unos mensajes
de Victoria.* Hablamos *del Real Madrid y de
fútbol.*

caro = *expensive*
compartimos = *we shared*
durante = *during*
recibió = *he received*

Gramática

The preterite of *-er* and *-ir* verbs

comer	*to eat*		salir	*to go out*
comí	*I ate*		salí	*I went out*
comiste	*you ate*		saliste	*you went out*
comió	*he/she ate*		salió	*he/she went out*
comimos	*we ate*		salimos	*we went out*
comisteis	*you (plural) ate*		salisteis	*you (plural) went out*
comieron	*they ate*		salieron	*they went out*

Para saber más página 132; ej. 11

leer **2** Lee el texto y contesta a las preguntas en inglés.

Ejemplo: **1** In Madrid.

1 Where did Alex have dinner with David Beckham?
2 When did he have dinner with David Beckham?
3 What did Alex eat?

4 What did David eat?
5 What did they drink?
6 What did they talk about?

leer 3 Lee el texto otra vez. Copia y rellena la tabla con los **verbos** del texto.

Preterite	English	Infinitive	English
salí	I went out	salir	to go out

Can you spot the preterite forms of these verbs in the exercise 1 text?
salir *(to go out)*
compartir *(to share)*
recibir *(to receive)*
comer *(to eat)*
beber *(to drink)*

 Escuchar 4 Escucha a Rosa y escribe la letra correcta.

Ejemplo: **1** a

1	Rosa went out with	**a** J-Lo	**b** Antonio Banderas.
2	She flew to	**a** Las Vegas	**b** Los Angeles.
3	They ate in	**a** a Spanish restaurant	**b** a Mexican restaurant.
4	Rosa ate	**a** salad	**b** prawns.
5	J-Lo ate	**a** soup	**b** salad.
6	They both had	**a** chicken	**b** paella.
7	Rosa's dessert was	**a** ice-cream	**b** crème caramel.
8	J-Lo had	**a** fruit	**b** crème caramel.
9	They drank	**a** lemonade	**b** Coke.
10	They talked about	**a** music	**b** football.

 hablar 5 Con tu compañero/a, pregunta y contesta sobre una cena.

- ¿Con quién saliste?
- Salí con …
- ¿Adónde fuiste?
- Fui a …
- ¿Qué comiste?
- Comí …
- ¿Qué bebiste?
- Bebí …
- ¿Cómo fue?
- Fue …

 escribir 6 Describe una cena con una persona famosa.

Mi cena con …
El fin de semana pasado salí con …
Fui a …
Fue …
De primer plato comí …
Mi compañero/a comió …
De segundo plato comí …
Mi compañero/a comió …
De postre comí …
Mi compañero/a comió …
Bebimos …
Hablamos de …
Fue …

5 ¿Qué te gusta comer?

● Talking about likes and dislikes
● Using past, present and future together

¿Quién habla? Escucha y escribe el nombre correcto. (1–4)

Ejemplo: **1** Juana

Elena

Juana

Rico

Ramón

¿Qué te gusta comer?		¿Qué te gusta beber?	
Me gusta comer A veces como Nunca como	magdalenas tostadas cereales patatas fritas pescado paella pollo gambas ensalada helado fruta	Me gusta beber Nunca bebo	agua limonada zumo de naranja Cola Cao Coca-Cola

Make sure you understand the difference:

Me gusta comer …   *I like to eat …*
Como …   *I eat …*

2 Con tu compañero/a, haz un diálogo.

● ¿Qué te gusta comer?
■ Me gusta comer … pero nunca como …
● ¿Qué te gusta beber?
■ Me gusta beber … pero nunca bebo …

3 Escucha y lee. Copia y rellena la tabla.

	Le gusta	No le gusta
Elisa	fruta, ensalada ...	
Alejandro		

Menú del día

moscas

cucarachas

arañas

gusanos

> Normalmente como mucha fruta y ensalada y bebo agua pero ayer comí arañas. ¡Qué horror! Y mañana voy a comer un bocadillo de moscas. ¡Ay! No puedo. Me gusta comer ensalada de lechuga y pepino … Quiero salir de aquí.

Elisa

> Normalmente como pasta. También me gusta comer nachos y hamburguesas. No quiero comer insectos. No me gustan nada. El fin de semana pasado bebí un cóctel de gusanos y mañana voy a comer cucarachas con mayonesa. ¡Buagh, qué asco!

Alejandro

4 Contesta a las preguntas en inglés para Elisa y Alejandro.

Ejemplo: **1** Elisa normally eats salad and fruit.

1 What do they normally eat?
2 What did they eat in the jungle?
3 What are they going to eat tomorrow?

5 Lee los textos otra vez. Escribe los verbos en la tabla.

Presente	Pretérito	Futuro
como		

Use the time expressions in the exercise 3 texts to help you.

normalmente
ayer
mañana

6 ¿Qué te gusta comer? Copia y completa la ficha.
Mira la sección Palabras (páginas 76 y 77).

Normalmente como

A veces como

Me gusta mucho comer

No me gusta nada comer

Nunca bebo

El fin de semana pasado comí

Mañana voy a comer

Resumen

Unidad 1

I can

- *say what I have for breakfast, lunch, tea and dinner* — Desayuno cereales. Como carne con verduras. Meriendo galletas. Ceno pollo.
- *say what I drink* — Bebo Cola Cao, té, zumo de naranja …
- *ask someone what they have for breakfast, lunch, tea and dinner* — ¿Qué desayunas? ¿Qué comes? ¿Qué meriendas? ¿Qué cenas?
- *ask someone what they drink* — ¿Qué bebes?
- *say at what time I have different meals* — Desayuno a las siete. Como a la una.
- *understand time expressions* — nunca, de vez en cuando, siempre, generalmente

Unidad 2

I can

- *use shopping phrases* — Un kilo de tomates, por favor. Nada más, gracias.
- *ask how much something costs* — ¿Cuánto cuesta?
- *say how much something costs* — Tres euros y cincuenta céntimos.
- *understand and use high numbers* — cien, ciento diez, quinientos, ochocientos, mil
- **G** *use expressions of quantity* — un kilo de peras, dos kilos de tomates, cien gramos de jar
- **G** *use the preterite to say what I bought* — **Fui** al mercado y **compré** un cartón de leche.

Unidad 3

I can

- *order in a restaurant* — De primer plato, quiero una ensalada. De segundo plato, quiero pollo. De postre, quiero un helado.
- *say what I'd like to drink* — Para beber, quiero una limonada.
- *say I'm hungry* — Tengo hambre.
- *say I'm thirsty* — Tengo sed.
- *ask for the bill* — La cuenta, por favor.
- **G** *spot verbs that go with* tú *and* usted — ¿Qué **vas** a tomar? ¿Qué **va** a tomar?

Unidad 4

I can

- **G** *use the preterite of* **-er** *and* **-ir** *verbs* — De postre **comí** un helado de chocolate. **Bebí** agua. Mi compañera no **comió** nada. **Compartimos** una pae

Unidad 5

I can

- *talk about what I like to eat and drink* — Me gusta comer magdalenas. A veces como tostadas. Nunca como cereales. Me gusta beber té.
- **G** *use three tenses together* — *(present)* Normalmente **como** fruta. Me **gusta** mucho comer ensalada. *(past)* El fin de semana pasado **comí** pollo y pizza. *(future)* Mañana **voy a comer** nachos y hamburguesas.

1 Escucha. Copia y rellena la tabla.

	Desayuno	Comida	Cena
Gustavo			
Rosa			
Enrique			

 2 Con tu compañero/a, haz diálogos.

- ¿Qué quieres?
- Quinientos gramos de jamón, por favor.
- ¿Algo más?
- Sí, … ¿Cuánto cuesta?
- Diez euros.

1 100g 1Kg 500g 500g 10€

2 2Kg 2Kg 500g 7,50€

3 3,20€

4 2,75€

 3 Lee y empareja las mitades de las frases. Escribe las frases completas en el orden correcto para hacer un diálogo.

1 ¿Para	quiero unas gambas. **a**
2 De primer plato	quiero pollo. **b**
3 De segundo plato	quiero un helado. **c**
4 De postre	va a tomar? **d**
5 ¿Qué	por favor. **e**
6 Agua,	beber? **f**

 **4** Escribe un correo. Incluye los datos siguientes.
Write an email. Include the following details.

- *Say what you normally eat for breakfast, lunch, tea and dinner.*
- *Say what you like to eat and drink.*
- *Say what you never eat.*
- *Say what you ate and drank yesterday.*
- *Say what you are going to have tomorrow.*

Normalmente desayuno …
como … meriendo … ceno …
Me gusta comer … y beber …
Nunca como …
Ayer comí … y bebí …
Mañana voy a tomar …

¡Extra! 1

1 **Escucha y elige el verbo correcto. Luego escribe las frases en inglés.**

1 Ayer Diego no **desayuno** / **desayunó** nada …
2 … pero **tomo** / **tomó** chocolate con dos kilos de churros a las dos de la tarde.
3 Luego **vomito** / **vomitó**.
4 **Bebo** / **Bebió** mucha agua …
5 … y más tarde **ceno** / **cenó** con su familia.

2 **¿Comes una dieta sana? ¡Compruébalo con este test!**
Do you have a healthy diet? Find out with this test!

¿Qué comes?

1 ¿Qué prefieres comer?
a Prefiero comer hamburguesas.
b Prefiero comer plátanos.

2 ¿Qué prefieres beber?
a Prefiero beber café.
b Prefiero beber agua.

3 ¿Qué comiste ayer?
a Comí una bolsa de patatas fritas.
b Comí una ensalada mixta.

4 ¿Qué bebiste ayer?
a Bebí una Coca-Cola.
b Bebí leche.

5 ¿Qué vas a desayunar mañana?
a Voy a desayunar chocolate con churros.
b Voy a desayunar fruta y agua.

6 ¿Qué vas a cenar mañana?
a Voy a cenar patatas fritas.
b Voy a cenar pescado con ensalada.

¡Ahora calcula!
a = 1 punto, **b** = 2 puntos

10–12 puntos: Comes una dieta muy sana. ¡Muy bien!

8–9 puntos: Comes una dieta bastante sana. Trata de elegir la opción sana todo el tiempo.

6–7 puntos Tu dieta no es sana. Tienes que comer fruta y verduras frecuentemente.

3 Escucha a Lola. Completa las frases.

1	Me gusta comer …	porque es/son	delicioso/a/os/as
2	No me gusta comer …	porque no es/no son	rico/a/os/as
3	Todos los días como …		sano/a/os/as
4	Algunas veces a la semana como …		grasiento/a/os/as
5	El fin de semana pasado comí …		
6	Mañana voy a comer …		

4 Pon los dibujos en el orden del texto.

Ejemplo: b, …

Normalmente desayuno a las siete y media. Desayuno tostadas y zumo de naranja.

Como a la una. Normalmente como pizza o pasta. Ceno a las nueve. De primer plato tomo sopa o ensalada, de segundo plato tomo pollo o pescado y de postre como fruta.

El fin de semana pasado salí con unos amigos. Fuimos a un restaurante español en Barcelona y cenamos juntos. De primer plato tomé gambas y de segundo plato tomé carne con patatas fritas. De postre comí un helado de fresa – ¡rico, rico, rico! Bebimos agua. Bailamos y cantamos en el restaurante. Lo pasamos muy bien.

Lidia

5 Prepara una presentación.

- *Say what you like to eat (page 68)*
- *Say what you like to drink (page 68)*
- *Say what you normally eat for breakfast (page 60)*
- *Say what you normally eat for lunch (page 60)*
- *Say what you normally eat for dinner (page 60)*
- *Say why (page 73)*
- *Say what you ate yesterday (page 66)*
- *Say what you are going to eat tomorrow (page 69)*

Make your sentences as interesting as possible:
- use 'but' (page 61)
- use 'sometimes', 'normally', … (page 61)
- say what you never eat (page 61)

 **Escucha y lee.**

1

P – Tengo hambre, Diego.
¿Vamos a comer algo?
D – De acuerdo. ¿Qué te
gusta comer?

2

P – A ver … me gusta mucho la carne.
Y me gusta mucho la fruta también,
sobre todo las uvas, las peras y los
plátanos. La fruta es rica y muy sana.

3

D – Ayer fui a la Boquería, allí tienen mucha fruta.
P – ¿La Boquería? ¿Qué es?
D – Es un mercado en las Ramblas de Barcelona.

4

D – Pero … ¡tengo una idea! Te invito a
ir de tapas y luego a comer paella.

5

C – ¿Qué van a tomar?
D – Una ración de aceitunas, una ración
de albóndigas y unas patatas bravas.

6

P – ¿Cuál es la comida típica de Barcelona?
D – La escalibada y la paella negra o de
marisco. La escalibada está hecha de
pimiento, berenjena y cebolla.

7

D – ¿Te gusta la paella, Patricia?
P – Hmm, está deliciosa …
Gracias por invitarme.
D – De nada, es un placer.

sobre todo = *above all*
ir de tapas = *to go for tapas (small bar snack*
una ración de = *a portion of*
aceitunas = *olives*
albóndigas = *meatballs*
patatas bravas = *spicy potatoes*
pimiento = *sweet pepper*
berenjena = *aubergine*
cebolla = *onion*

 2 Con tu compañero/a, lee en voz alta la historia de Patricia y Diego.

Termina estas frases.

1 A Patricia le gusta comer …
2 Ayer Diego fue …
3 La Boquería es …
4 Diego y Patricia toman una ración de …, … y …
5 La comida típica de Barcelona es …
6 La escalibada está hecha de …

Empareja las personas con los restaurantes.

1 *Quiero ir a un restaurante italiano.*

2 *No tengo mucha hambre. ¿Podemos ir de tapas?*

3 *No como carne. Prefiero el pescado.*

4 *No como mariscos. Tengo alergia.*

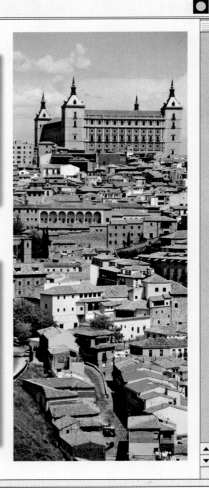

www.toledo.es/restaurantes

a El Cantábrico

En El Cantábrico hay más de 10 clases de pescado y marisco diferentes. Los entrantes (pulpo, verdura frita, …) y los arroces tampoco te los puedes perder.

b Cervecería La Barra

La tapa es, sin duda, la especialidad de esta casa. Preparan hasta 150 tapas diferentes aunque las más famosas son las de anchoa, jamón, atún y lomo. Todo un lujo.

c El Albero

En El Albero vas a disfrutar de una deliciosa carne roja preparada a la piedra. También sirven una deliciosa perdiz estofada y rabo de toro. Son sólo tres sugerencias de su variada carta.

d Alfil

Restaurante típico italiano en el interior de Toledo. Además de exquisitas pizzas ofrecen una gran variedad de platos italianos y todo tipo de pastas. También hay ensaladas variadas y sándwiches. Platos para todos los gustos.

***Choose two restaurants and write lists of what they offer. To help you, first look up the underlined words in the* Vocabulario.**

Palabras

Las comidas	**Meals**
¿Qué desayunas?	*What do you eat for breakfast?*
¿Qué comes?	*What do you eat for lunch?*
¿Qué meriendas?	*What do you eat for tea?*
¿Qué cenas?	*What do you eat for supper/dinner?*
Desayuno …	*For breakfast I eat …*
Como …	*For lunch I eat …*
Meriendo …	*For tea I eat …*
Ceno …	*For supper/dinner I eat …*
carne con verduras	*meat with vegetables*
cereales	*cereal*
fruta	*fruit*
galletas	*biscuits*
magdalenas	*fairy cakes*
pasta	*pasta*
patatas fritas	*chips*
pescado con ensalada	*fish with salad*
pizza	*pizza*
pollo	*chicken*
tostadas	*toast*
un bocadillo	*a sandwich*
¿Qué bebes?	*What do you drink?*
Bebo …	*I drink …*
Cola Cao	*Cola Cao (drinking chocolate)*
té	*tea*
zumo de naranja	*orange juice*
No meriendo.	*I don't have tea.*
No desayuno nada.	*I don't have anything for breakfast.*
Nunca como.	*I never have lunch.*
¿A qué hora desayunas/cenas?	*At what time do you have breakfast/dinner?*
Desayuno a las ocho.	*I have breakfast at eight o'clock.*
Como a mediodía.	*I have lunch at midday.*
Ceno después de las nueve.	*I have dinner after nine o'clock.*
siempre	*always*
generalmente	*usually*

normalmente	*normally*
a veces	*sometimes*
de vez en cuando	*from time to time*
todo el tiempo	*all the time*

Los números	**Numbers**
cien	*100*
ciento diez	*110*
doscientos	*200*
trescientos	*300*
cuatrocientos	*400*
quinientos	*500*
seiscientos	*600*
setecientos	*700*
ochocientos	*800*
novecientos	*900*
mil	*1000*

En el mercado	**At the market**
¿Qué quieres?	*What would you like?*
un kilo de …	*a kilo of …*
dos kilos de …	*two kilos of …*
medio kilo de …	*half a kilo of …*
quinientos gramos de …	*500 grams of …*
jamón	*ham*
manzanas	*apples*
peras	*pears*
queso	*cheese*
tomates	*tomatoes*
uvas	*grapes*
zanahorias	*carrots*
un cartón de leche	*a carton of milk*
un chorizo	*a chorizo (spicy Spanish sausage)*
una barra de pan	*a baguette/loaf of bread*
una botella de agua	*a bottle of water*
una lechuga	*a lettuce*
¿Algo más?	*Anything else?*
Sí, quiero …	*Yes, I'd like …*
por favor	*please*
Nada más, gracias.	*Nothing else, thanks.*
¿Cuánto cuesta?	*How much is it?*
Un euro.	*One euro.*
Dos euros y veinte céntimos.	*€2,20.*
Ochenta céntimos.	*Eighty cents.*

En el restaurante — At the restaurant

¿Qué vas/va a tomar?	What are you (familiar/ polite) going to have?
De primer plato …	As a starter …
De segundo plato …	As a main course …
De postre …	As a dessert …
quiero …	I'd like …
fruta	fruit
pescado	fish
pollo	chicken
un flan	a crème caramel
un helado (de chocolate)	a (chocolate) ice-cream
una ensalada	a salad
una paella (de mariscos)	a (seafood) paella
una sopa	a soup
unas gambas	some prawns
¿Para beber?	And to drink?
(Quiero) …, por favor.	(I want/I'd like) …, please.
agua	water
una Coca-Cola	a Coca-Cola
una limonada	a lemonade
Tengo hambre.	I'm hungry.
No tengo hambre.	I'm not hungry.
Tengo sed.	I'm thirsty.
La cuenta, por favor.	The bill, please.

Una cena especial — A special dinner

El fin de semana pasado …	Last weekend …
salí con …	I went out with …
Fui a …	I went to …
un restaurante español	a Spanish restaurant
un restaurante muy caro	a very expensive restaurant
Comí una ensalada.	I ate a salad.
Mi compañero/a comió gambas.	My companion ate prawns.
Compartimos una paella.	We shared a paella.
Bebimos agua.	We drank water.
Hablamos de fútbol/ música.	We talked about football/music.
¡Fue genial!	It was brilliant!

¿Qué te gusta comer? — What do you like eating?

Me gusta (mucho) comer …	I (really) like eating …
No me gusta (nada) comer …	I don't like eating … (at all).
A veces como …	I sometimes eat …
Nunca como …	I never eat …
Me gusta beber …	I like drinking …
Nunca bebo …	I never drink …
Normalmente como …	Normally I eat …
El fin de semana pasado comí …	Last weekend I ate …
Mañana voy a comer …	Tomorrow I'm going to eat …

Palabras muy útiles — Very useful words

normalmente	normally
de	of, about
nada	nothing
nunca	never
algo	anything, something
mucho/a/os/as	a lot of

Estrategia

Finding the right word

Be careful not to choose the wrong Spanish word when you use a dictionary. For example, someone wanted to say *I drink tea* and ended up with **Bebo merienda**. Why is this wrong?

Here are ways of avoiding this kind of mistake:

1 Make sure you look up the correct spelling of the English word (e.g. meat/meet, pear/pair).
2 Look for dictionary abbreviations (*vt, nm, nf,* etc. – see page 41). If it's a noun you want, don't choose a verb (e.g. a drink/to drink).
3 Look at any example sentences given.
4 Double-check the Spanish word in the Spanish–English half of the dictionary.

Find the correct Spanish translations of these foods in a dictionary (they all have double meanings or more than one spelling!):

jam   roll   bean
sweet   cake   chop

¿Qué llevas?

Normalmente llevo ...

escuchar 1 Escucha y escribe las letras de la ropa mencionada. (1–6)

Ejemplo: **1** f, h

a un jersey

b un vestido

c una falda

d una gorra

e una camisa

f una camiseta

g una sudadera

h unos vaqueros

i unos pantalones

j unos zapatos

k unas botas

l unas zapatillas de deporte

escuchar 2 Escucha. ¿Qué llevan?
Contesta en inglés. (1–5)

Ejemplo: **1** jeans,
sweatshirt,
baseball cap

Gramática

Singular		Plural	
masculine	**feminine**	**masculine**	**feminine**
un vestido	una gorra	unos zapatos	unas botas
a dress	a cap	some shoes	some boots

Para saber más | página 127

escuchar 3 Escucha otra vez. Escribe la expresión de frecuencia para cada artículo. (1–5)
Write down the frequency expression you hear for each item.

Ejemplo: **1** jeans, sweatshirt – normalmente; baseball cap – siempre

nunca	de vez en cuando	a veces	a menudo	normalmente	siempre
never	*from time to time*	*sometimes*	*often*	*normally*	*always*

4 Con tu compañero/a, haz diálogos.

● ¿Qué llevas <u>siempre</u>?
■ <u>Siempre</u> llevo …

> siempre
> normalmente
> nunca
> a veces
> de vez en cuando
> a menudo

Gramática

	Singular		Plural	
	masculine	**feminine**	**masculine**	**feminine**
	rojo	roja	rojos	rojas
	negro	negra	negros	negras
	marrón	marrón	marrones	marrones
	verde	verde	verdes	verdes

Para saber más   página 127

 5 Escucha y lee. Luego pon las personas en el grupo apropiado. (1–6)

Ejemplo: **Pepe** – f

Las tribus urbanas. ¿En qué grupo estás tú?

a Los skaters **b Los raperos** **c Los pijos** **d Los heavies** **e Los lolailos** **f Los punkis**

Pepe

Siempre llevo unos vaqueros negros y unas botas negras. Me encanta la música de los Sex Pistols y los piercings.

Sergio

Normalmente llevo una camiseta gris muy grande, unos vaqueros y una gorra azul. Me gustan **las joyas preciosas**.

Marco

Normalmente llevo una camiseta **sin mangas**, unos vaqueros y unas botas altas. Me encanta Kiss. Odio a los pijos.

Ana

A menudo llevo una camiseta blanca, un jersey rojo y unos vaqueros **de marca**. Me encanta el dinero. Odio a los heavies.

Ricardo

Siempre llevo una camisa blanca. Tengo el pelo largo y rizado. A veces llevo **gafas de sol**. Me gusta bailar. Me encanta **el ritmo**. ¡Olé!

Lola

Llevo una sudadera amarilla, unos vaqueros y unas zapatillas de deporte. De vez en cuando llevo **una muñequera**. Me gusta mucho ir al parque con mis amigos.

 6 ¿Qué significan las palabras en azul en los textos? Utiliza el contexto.

7 ¿En qué grupo estás tú? Contesta a la pregunta y describe tu estilo.

1 Escucha y escribe la letra correcta. (1–8)

Ejemplo: **1** e

a Este jersey es feo.

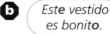

b Este vestido es bonito.

c Esta chaqueta es cómoda.

d Esta corbata es anticuada.

e Esta camiseta es guay.

f Estos pantalones son baratos.

g Estos zapatos son incómodos.

h Estas botas son caras.

Gramática

this/these

Singular		Plural	
masculine	**feminine**	**masculine**	**feminine**
est**e** vestido *this dress*	est**a** chaqueta *this jacket*	est**os** zapatos *these shoes*	est**as** botas *these boots*

Para saber más página 129; ej. 3

2 Empareja los antónimos.
Match up the opposites.

Ejemplo: barato – caro

dofeoincómo docaroguay
bonitocómodo baratoanticua

3 Describe la ropa de tu profesor/profesora.

● Esta corbata es anticuada …

4 **Escucha y lee. Contesta a las preguntas para cada persona.**

- ¿Lleva uniforme?
- ¿Le gusta el uniforme?

> In Spain most pupils don't wear school uniform, but pupils at private schools often do.

¿te gusta el uniforme?

En mi colegio tengo que llevar uniforme. No me gusta nada porque es anticuado, feo y muy incómodo. También es caro. Prefiero la ropa de los fines de semana: vaqueros, una sudadera y zapatillas de deporte. Es más cómoda.
Alejandro

Yo no llevo uniforme. Normalmente para ir al colegio llevo una camiseta, unos vaqueros y zapatillas de deporte. Esta ropa es más cómoda que una corbata y una chaqueta.
Belén

Tengo que llevar uniforme. Llevo una falda, un jersey, una camisa, una corbata y una chaqueta. Me gusta llevar uniforme. Es más práctico para ir al colegio. También es más elegante, pero a veces es menos cómodo.
Marisol

> para ir al colegio = *for going to school*

5 **Lee los textos otra vez. Corrige las frases.**

Ejemplo: **1** A Alejandro no le gusta llevar uniforme.

1 A Alejandro le gusta llevar uniforme.
2 No le gusta nada el uniforme porque es bonito y cómodo.
3 Belén lleva uniforme.
4 Para ir al colegio, lleva una corbata y una chaqueta.
5 Marisol lleva vaqueros y una camiseta.
6 A Marisol no le gusta llevar uniforme.

Gramática

Comparatives

más … que	*more … than*
menos … que	*less … than*

List the comparatives in the texts above.

6 **Haz este sondeo en tu clase.**

Uniforme – ¿Sí o no?

1 Llevar uniforme es más práctico que llevar vaqueros.
2 Llevar zapatillas de deporte para ir al colegio es más cómodo que llevar zapatos.
3 Llevar camisa es menos cómodo que llevar camiseta.
4 Llevar uniforme es más incómodo que llevar vaqueros.
5 Llevar vaqueros es menos elegante que llevar uniforme.

7 **Escribe lo que llevas para ir al colegio.**

Para ir al colegio, normalmente llevo … . También llevo …
(No) Me gusta porque es …
Es más … que … . Es menos … que …

3 ¿Qué prefieres?

1 Escucha las preguntas y escribe la letra correcta. (1–8)
(For questions 5–8 you need to give your own opinion.)

¿Qué vestido es **el** más …?

¿Qué camiseta es **la** más …?

Ejemplo: **1** c

¿Qué pantalones son **los** más …?

¿Qué botas son **las** más …?

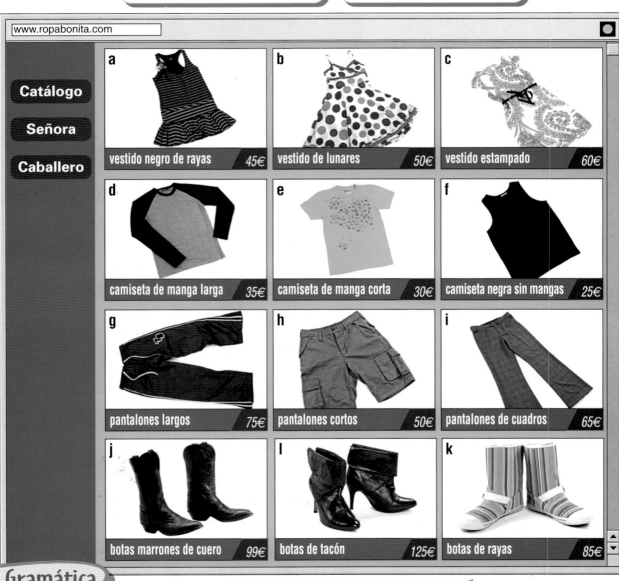

www.ropabonita.com

Catálogo

Señora

Caballero

a vestido negro de rayas 45€	**b** vestido de lunares 50€	**c** vestido estampado 60€
d camiseta de manga larga 35€	**e** camiseta de manga corta 30€	**f** camiseta negra sin mangas 25€
g pantalones largos 75€	**h** pantalones cortos 50€	**i** pantalones de cuadros 65€
j botas marrones de cuero 99€	**l** botas de tacón 125€	**k** botas de rayas 85€

Gramática

Superlatives

est**e** vestido es **el más cómodo**	*this dress is **the most comfortable***
est**a** camiseta es **la menos bonita**	*this T-shirt is **the least attractive***
est**os** pantalones son **los más baratos**	*these trousers are **the cheapest***
est**as** botas son **las menos prácticas**	*these boots are **the least practical***

Para saber más

página 128; ej. 2

2 **Con tu compañero/a, pregunta y contesta sobre cada sección del catálogo.**

- ¿Qué vestido es el más caro?
- ¿Qué camiseta es la más cara?
- ¿Qué pantalones son los más caros?
- ¿Qué botas son las más caras?

- ¿Qué vestido es el menos guay?
- ¿Qué camiseta es la menos guay?
- ¿Qué pantalones son los menos guays?
- ¿Qué botas son las menos guays?

 3 **Escribe seis preguntas y respuestas sobre los artículos del catálogo.**

> *Ejemplo:* ¿Qué vestido es el más barato?
> El vestido negro de rayas es el más barato.

 4 **Escucha y lee.**

- Quiero comprar una chaqueta.
  ¿Cuál prefieres? ¿La naranja o la roja?
- Me gusta esta chaqueta naranja con botones negros. Es la más barata.
- Sí, voy a comprar la chaqueta naranja.

| ¿Cuál? | Which one? |
| ¿Cuáles? | Which ones? |

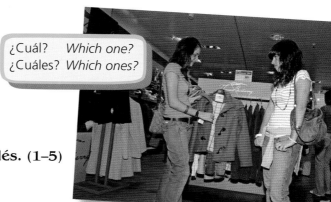

 5 **Escucha. Copia y rellena la tabla en inglés. (1–5)**

	Article bought	Reason bought
1	green dress	most elegant

 6 **Escucha y completa el texto de la canción. (1–8)**

> *Ejemplo:* **1** este

Ir de compras

¿Te gusta ⁽¹⁾ jersey violeta?
No me gusta nada, prefiero esta ⁽²⁾ .
Estos vaqueros son ⁽³⁾ ,
pero me gustan porque son estampados.
Ir de compras, ir de compras, siempre un placer.

¿Te gusta este vestido de flores?
Pues no, prefiero la falda de muchos colores.
¿Te gustan ⁽⁴⁾ zapatos de cuero?
Prefiero ⁽⁵⁾ botas, valen menos dinero.
Ir de compras, ir de compras, siempre un placer.

⁽⁶⁾ corbata negra es muy ⁽⁷⁾ .
Yo prefiero la de lunares. Me gusta bastante.
¿Cuál prefieres? ¿La camisa ⁽⁸⁾ o la camiseta?
Voy a comprar las dos, y también la sudadera.
Ir de compras, ir de compras, siempre un placer.

un placer = *a pleasure*
de flores = *flowery*
valen = *they cost*

Mini-test

I can
- say what I always/normally/sometimes/never wear
- give an opinion on items of clothing
- compare school uniform with casual clothes
- say which items of clothing are the most expensive, cheapest, etc.
- **G** make adjectives agree
- **G** use **este**, **esta**, **estos** and **estas**
- **G** use comparatives and superlatives

1 Escucha y lee. Elige la frase apropiada para terminar cada texto. Escribe la letra correcta. (1–3)

ARGENTINA

Buenos Aires

Chapelco

Mar del Plata

El Calafate

1

¿Qué tal? Me llamo Miguel. Soy estadounidense. Estoy de vacaciones en Chapelco con mi hermano. Me encanta Argentina, es un país muy bonito. El fútbol es mi deporte favorito. Me encanta ver partidos de fútbol.

Normalmente llevo ropa de deporte. Llevo una camiseta, vaqueros y zapatillas de deporte. A veces llevo una gorra. ¡Mañana voy a hacer esquí, entonces voy a llevar algo diferente! …

2

¡Buen día! ¿Qué tal? Me llamo Alba. Soy mexicana. Estoy de vacaciones en Mar del Plata. La gente argentina es muy simpática. En mi tiempo libre me encanta jugar a los videojuegos y chatear por internet. Aquí en Argentina no tengo ordenador.

Normalmente llevo una falda con una camiseta y zapatillas de deporte. Pero mañana por la mañana voy a tomar el sol en la playa …

3

¡Hola! ¿Cómo estás? Me llamo Rodrigo. Soy chileno. Estoy de vacaciones en El Calafate. Me encanta leer cómics. Tengo una colección de cómics de Astérix.

Normalmente llevo un jersey y unos vaqueros. Es ropa cómoda y práctica. No me interesa la moda. Mañana voy a ir al Perito Moreno en barco. Es un glaciar. No puedo llevar mi ropa habitual.

a Voy a llevar un vestido rojo sin mangas y zapatos negros de tacón.
b Voy a llevar mucha ropa: botas, pantalones, chaqueta y gafas.
c Voy a llevar unas botas, unos pantalones, unas gafas, una chaqueta y los esquís, por supuesto.
d Voy a llevar un bañador y mis gafas de sol.

algo = *something*
glaciar = *glacier*
esquís = *skis*
bañador = *swimsuit*

2 Lee los textos. ¿Verdadero (V), falso (F) o no se sabe (NS)?
¿True, false or not known?

1 Miguel likes Argentina because it's famous for football.
2 Miguel likes to play football.
3 Alba finds Argentinian people unfriendly.

4 She likes reading.
5 Rodrigo likes reading at home.
6 He's very interested in fashion.

 3 Lee otra vez. Copia y rellena la tabla en español.

	Normalmente lleva …	Mañana va a …	Va a llevar …
Miguel	*una camiseta, …*		
Alba			
Rodrigo			

 4 Escucha y contesta a las preguntas en inglés para cada persona. (1–5)

1 Where do they come from?
2 Where are they going on holiday?
3 What are they going to do there?
4 What do they normally wear?
5 What are they going to wear?

 5 Pon las palabras en el orden correcto. Traduce las preguntas al inglés.

Ejemplo: **1** ¿Cómo te llamas? – What are you called?

1 ¿Cómo llamas? te
2 años ¿Cuántos tienes?
3 ¿Cuál tu nacionalidad? es
4 ¿Qué gusta? te

5 tiempo tu en libre? haces ¿Qué
6 llevas ¿Qué normalmente?
7 hacer ¿Qué mañana? a vas
8 vas llevar? a ¿Qué

 6 Con tu compañero/a, pregunta y contesta por Javier. Utiliza las preguntas del ejercicio 5.

● ¿Cómo te llamas?
■ Me llamo Javier.

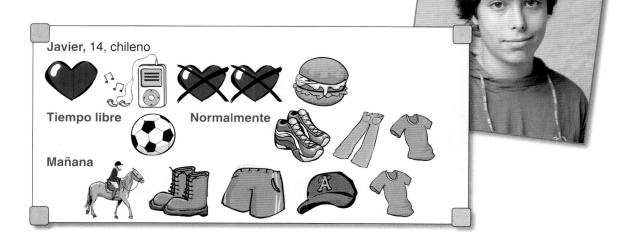

Javier, 14, chileno

Tiempo libre

Normalmente

Mañana

escuchar 1 Escucha y lee el texto de Dolores.

Ayer **salí** con mis amigos y **fuimos** a un baile de disfraces. Yo **llevé** un vestido de princesa y **fue** muy divertido porque normalmente **llevo** vaqueros y una camiseta de fútbol todo el tiempo. **Me encanta** el fútbol, **juego** mucho, soy muy buena.

En el baile **comí** ensalada y tortilla. **Bebí** limonada. Lo **pasé** guay. Fue muy, muy divertido.

La próxima vez **voy a llevar** unas botas, una camisa blanca muy larga y un sombrero rojo: **voy a ser** pirata del Caribe.

Dolores

Train yourself to spot different tenses:

Past	Present	Future
salí	llevo	voy a llevar
fuimos	me encanta	voy a ser

leer 2 Busca estos verbos en el texto.

1	I wear	**6**	I am going to be
2	I ate	**7**	I drank
3	I went out	**8**	I wore
4	it was	**9**	I am going to wear
5	we went	**10**	I love

hablar 3 Con tu compañero/a, traduce las frases al español.

Ejemplo: **1** Ayer salí con mis padres.

1 Yesterday I went out with my parents.
2 We went to a restaurant.
3 It was great.
4 I ate salad, chicken and ice-cream.
5 Next time I am going to eat paella.
6 I wore jeans and a T-shirt.
7 Normally I wear trousers and a sweatshirt all the time.

> You can use the text above to help you: it contains phrases that you can adapt by changing a few words each time.

escuchar 4 Escucha y contesta a las preguntas por Eva y César. (1–2)

a ¿Qué llevaste para ir al baile?
b ¿Qué llevas normalmente?
c ¿Qué vas a llevar la próxima vez?

gótica = *goth*
momia = *mummy*

leer 5 Lee los textos. Empareja los dibujos con las personas.

Ejemplo: **1** Juanita

Mi amiga Rosa fue de bruja. Llevó un vestido negro y un sombrero negro muy largo.

Ángel fue de vampiro. Llevó una capa negra y unos pantalones negros con una camisa blanca.

Luisa fue de policía. Llevó el uniforme normal: una gorra, una chaqueta, una falda y unos zapatos negros.

A Juanita le gusta Caperucita. Llevó una capa roja con una falda roja también.

Carlos fue de vaquero pero sin caballo. Llevó sus vaqueros, un sombrero y una camisa roja.

 leer 6 Elige el verbo correcto.

1 ¡Qué miedo! Ayer Rosa **lleva / llevó** ropa negra, un vestido, un sombrero y bigote.
2 Mañana Ángel también **llevó / va a llevar** unos dientes blancos largos, una capa negra, unos pantalones negros y una camisa blanca.
3 Luisa llevó un uniforme, ella **fue / va** de policía.
4 Carlos **llevo / llevó** vaqueros, un sombrero y una camisa.
5 A Juanita **le gusta / no le gusta** Caperucita.

 escribir 7 Copia las preguntas de la página web y completa las respuestas.

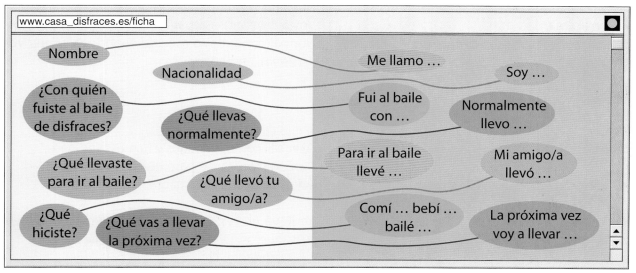

Resumen

Unidad 1

I can

- say what I wear
- **G** use adverbs of frequency to describe how often I wear items of clothing
- **G** use **unos/unas** (some)
- **G** make colour adjectives agree

Llevo una camiseta y unas botas.
A menudo llevo unos vaqueros.
De vez en cuando llevo una gorra.
Llevo **unos** pantalones y **unas** botas.
Siempre llevo un**os** vaquer**os** negr**os** y un**a** camis**a** b

Unidad 2

I can

- describe my school uniform
- say what I think about uniform
- **G** use **este**, **esta**, **estos**, **estas** (this/these)
- **G** use comparative adjectives

Para ir al colegio llevo una falda, un jersey y una chac
No me gusta nada porque es feo y muy incómodo.
Este vestido es bonito. **Estas** botas son caras.
Llevar uniforme es **más elegante** que llevar vaquer
Llevar camisa es **menos cómodo** que llevar camise

Unidad 3

I can

- ask someone which item of clothing they prefer
- say which item of clothing I like and why
- **G** use superlative adjectives

¿Cuál prefieres? ¿La naranja o la roja?

Me gusta esta chaqueta naranja. Es la más barata.
¿Qué vestido es **el más caro**?
Las botas de rayas son **las menos guays**.

Unidad 4

I can

- ask someone what they are going to do and what they will wear
- say what I'm going to do and what I shall wear
- **G** use the present and near future tenses together

¿Qué vas a hacer mañana?
¿Qué vas a llevar?
Mañana voy a montar a caballo.
Voy a llevar unas zapatillas de deporte y una chaqu
Normalmente **llevo** ropa de deporte. Mañana **voy**
    llevar un bañador.

Unidad 5

I can

- describe an event in the past

- describe what a friend wore to a fancy dress ball
- **G** use past, present and future tenses together

Ayer salí con mis amigos y fuimos a un baile.
    Comí tortilla. Lo pasé guay.
Ángel llevó una capa negra. Fue de vampiro.

Yo **llevé** un vestido de princesa. Normalmente **llevo**
    vaqueros. La próxima vez **voy a llevar** un
    sombrero rojo.

Prepárate

escuchar 1 Escucha y elige las dos cosas que menciona cada persona. (1–5)

Ejemplo: **1** a, g

hablar 2 Con tu compañero/a, haz frases sobre José, Juan y Xavier.

70€ José

50€ Juan

100€ Xavier

1 La ropa de José es más … que la ropa de …
2 La ropa de José es menos … que la ropa de …
3 La ropa de Juan es más … que la ropa de …
4 La ropa de Xavier es menos … que la ropa de …

5 José es el más …
6 Juan es el más …
7 Xavier es el más …

leer 3 Escribe las letras de la ropa que menciona Raúl.

Ejemplo: d, …

Tengo que llevar uniforme en el cole. Llevo unos pantalones negros, un jersey gris, una camisa blanca, una corbata y una chaqueta gris. Me gusta llevar uniforme porque es práctico para ir al colegio, pero no es muy cómodo. Tengo que llevar zapatos, y no me gusta nada. Prefiero llevar zapatillas de deporte.

Raúl

escribir 4 Escribe un texto sobre tu uniforme. Utiliza el texto del ejercicio 3 como modelo.

Escucha. ¿Quién habla? (1–5)

Ejemplo: **1** Juanita

Elena   **David**   **Montse**   **Eduardo**   **Juanita**   **Paco**

 Escucha otra vez. Elige la ropa apropiada para cada persona. (1–5)

El rojo El verde El marrón	me queda	bien mal
Mi color favorito es	el amarillo el azul el rosa	

Hablar **3** Con tu compañero/a, haz este test sobre la moda.

¿Tienes estilo?

1 Vas al casino. ¿Qué vas a llevar?
a Voy a llevar un vestido sin mangas / un traje elegante.
b Voy a llevar unos pantalones cortos rosa, con una camiseta naranja.

2 Llevar calcetines blancos y zapatos …
a no es guay.
b es guay.

3 Prefiero …
a la ropa cómoda.
b la ropa elegante.

4 Ayer fuiste al campo. ¿Qué llevaste?
a Llevé un vestido negro y zapatos de tacón / traje y corbata.
b Llevé unos pantalones cortos, una camiseta y zapatillas de deporte.

5 Cuando voy a la playa, llevo …
a unos pantalones de lunares y una camiseta de manga larga.
b un bañador y mis gafas de sol negras.

6 Vas a la bolera. ¿Qué vas a llevar?
a Voy a llevar unos vaqueros y una camiseta.
b Voy a llevar un traje de cuero negro.

7 Llevar la gorra al revés …
a es guay.
b no es guay.

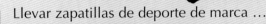

8 Llevar zapatillas de deporte de marca …
a es muy importante para mí.
b no es importante para mí.

¡Ahora calcula!	8–10 puntos:	11–13 puntos:	14–16 puntos:
1 a = 2, b = 1	Tu estilo de vestir es extravagante. Quizás eres un genio como Einstein o Mozart, pero por favor ¡no debes llevar calcetines blancos con zapatos!	La moda no es muy importante en tu vida pero tienes tu propio estilo y tus propias ideas. Eres interesante y divertido/a como María Sharapova o Roger Federer.	¡Relájate un poco! Eres un esclavo de la moda. Tus ídolos son David Beckham, Por favor, trata de ser un poco más independiente.
2 a = 2, b = 1			
3 a = 1, b = 2			
4 a = 2, b = 1			
5 a = 1, b = 2			
6 a = 1, b = 2			
7 a = 1, b = 2			
8 a = 2, b = 1			

Escribir **4** Copia y rellena este pasaporte de moda.

Tengo el pelo …
Tengo los ojos …
Normalmente llevo …
Me gusta la ropa …
Mi color favorito es el …
Mi diseñador favorito es …
Este fin de semana voy a …
Voy a llevar …

Escribir **5** Lee el pasaporte de moda de tu compañero/a y diseña algo para él/ella.

Escucha y lee. ❶

D – *Te gusta mucho el dibujo, Patricia, ¿verdad?*
P – *Sí, me encanta, me encanta. También me gusta ir de compras. Soy 'fashionista'. ¿Cuál es tu marca favorita, Diego?*

❷

D – *A ver, me gusta la ropa de Tommy Hilfiger y de Nike. ¿Quién es tu diseñador favorito?*

❸

P – *Bueno … me gusta mucho Stella McCartney. Es genial. Pero yo misma diseño unas cosas de vez en cuando. ¡Mira! ¡Tengo unas ideas para tu guardarropa!*

❹

D – *¡Es chulo! Me gusta muchísimo.*
P – *¿Vamos a mirar escaparates un poco?*

❺

P – *¡Qué guay! Me encantan estas zapatillas azules y amarillas. No son caras y son superchulas.*

❻

D – *Tenemos mucho en común, Patricia, ¿verdad?*
P – *Sí, Diego, tenemos mucho en común …*

yo mismo/a = *I myself*
diseñar = *to design*
chulo = *wicked*
mirar escaparates = *to go window-shopping*
tener mucho en común = *to have a lot in common*

2 Con tu compañero/a, lee en voz alta la historia de Patricia y Diego.

3 Copia y completa las frases.

1 A Patricia le gusta el dibujo e …
2 Las marcas favoritas de Diego son …
3 La diseñadora favorita de Patricia es …

4 Ella misma diseña …
5 Van a mirar …
6 Tienen mucho …

4 Copia y completa el texto.

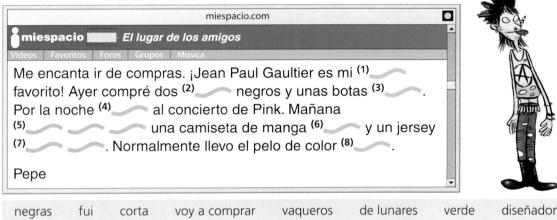

miespacio.com

miespacio *El lugar de los amigos*

Vídeos | Favoritos | Foros | Grupos | Música

Me encanta ir de compras. ¡Jean Paul Gaultier es mi (1) ____
favorito! Ayer compré dos (2) ____ negros y unas botas (3) ____.
Por la noche (4) ____ al concierto de Pink. Mañana
(5) ____ una camiseta de manga (6) ____ y un jersey
(7) ____. Normalmente llevo el pelo de color (8) ____.

Pepe

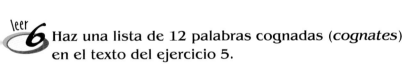

| negras | fui | corta | voy a comprar | vaqueros | de lunares | verde | diseñador |

5 Pon las frases en el orden correcto. Luego escucha y comprueba tus respuestas.

Ejemplo: c, …

a … los gauchos que habitaron las llanuras argentinas.
b … tipo de abrigo. Hay muchos …
c Un poncho consiste en un trozo de lana rectangular con abertura central. Es un …
d … poncho era parte de la vestimenta habitual de los nativos amerindios de la región. Fue esencial para …
e … diseños y colores diferentes. De origen andino, el …

6 Haz una lista de 12 palabras cognadas (*cognates*) en el texto del ejercicio 5.

7 Traduce el texto del ejercicio 5 al inglés.

Palabras

La ropa / **Clothes**

¿Qué llevas?	What do you wear?
Llevo …	I wear …
un jersey	a jumper
un vestido	a dress
una camisa	a shirt
una camiseta	a T-shirt
una falda	a skirt
una gorra	a cap
una sudadera	a sweatshirt
unos pantalones	trousers
unos vaqueros	jeans
unos zapatos	shoes
unas botas	boots
unas zapatillas de deporte	trainers

nunca	never
de vez en cuando	from time to time
a veces	sometimes
a menudo	often
normalmente	normally
siempre	always

Los colores / **Colours**

amarillo/a	yellow
blanco/a	white
negro/a	black
rojo/a	red
azul	blue
gris	grey
marrón	brown
naranja	orange
rosa	pink
verde	green

El uniforme escolar / **School uniform**

este jersey	this jumper
este vestido	this dress
esta camiseta	this T-shirt
esta chaqueta	this jacket
esta corbata	this tie
estos pantalones	these trousers
estos zapatos	these shoes
estas botas	these boots

anticuado/a	old-fashioned, out of date
barato/a	cheap
bonito/a	nice, pretty
caro/a	expensive
cómodo/a	comfortable
feo/a	ugly
guay	great, cool
incómodo/a	uncomfortable

Esta chaqueta es cómoda.	This jacket is comfortable.
Estos zapatos son incómodos.	These shoes are uncomfortable.

Tengo que llevar uniforme.	I have to wear a uniform.
No llevo uniforme.	I don't wear a uniform.

Para ir al colegio, normalmente llevo …	For school, I normally wear …
También llevo …	I also wear …
(No) Me gusta llevar uniforme.	I (don't) like wearing uniform.
Me gusta porque es práctico.	I like it because it's practical.
No me gusta porque es incómodo.	I don't like it because it's uncomfortable.
Es más elegante que llevar vaqueros.	It's more elegant/ stylish than wearing jeans.

¿Qué prefieres? / **What do you prefer?**

¿Qué vestido es el más …?	Which dress is the most …?
¿Qué camiseta es la menos …?	Which T-shirt is the least …?
¿Qué zapatos son los más …?	Which shoes are the most …?
¿Qué botas son las menos …?	Which boots are the least …?
Este vestido es el más bonito.	This dress is the nicest.
Esta camiseta es la menos cómoda.	This T-shirt is the least comfortable.

Estos zapatos son los más baratos.	*These shoes are the cheapest.*
Estas botas son las menos prácticas.	*These boots are the least practical.*
de cuadros	*checked*
de lunares	*spotted*
de rayas	*striped*
estampado/a	*patterned*
de manga corta	*short-sleeved*
de manga larga	*long-sleeved*
sin mangas	*sleeveless*
corto/a	*short*
largo/a	*long*
de cuero	*leather*
de tacón	*high-heeled*
¿Cuál prefieres?	*Which one do you prefer?*
¿Cuáles prefieres?	*Which ones do you prefer?*

Cuando estoy de vacaciones …	***When I'm on holiday …***
Normalmente llevo …	*Normally I wear …*
ropa de deporte	*sports clothes*
ropa cómoda	*comfortable clothes*
Mañana voy a llevar …	*Tomorrow I'm going to wear …*
un bañador	*swimsuit*
esquís	*skis*
mis gafas de sol	*my sunglasses*

Un baile de disfraces	***A fancy dress ball***
Ayer …	*Yesterday …*
salí con mis amigos	*I went out with friends*
fuimos a un baile de disfraces	*we went to a fancy dress ball*
Llevé …	*I wore …*
Bebí limonada.	*I drank lemonade.*
Bailé.	*I danced.*
Comí ensalada y tortilla.	*I ate salad and Spanish omelette.*
Llevé un vestido de princesa.	*I wore a princess dress.*
Fui de bruja.	*I went as a witch.*

Mi amigo/a fue de vampiro.	*My friend went as a vampire.*
Llevó …	*He/She wore …*
Fue muy divertido.	*It was very amusing/ entertaining.*
Normalmente llevo …	*Normally I wear…*
La próxima vez voy a llevar …	*Next time I'm going to wear …*

Palabras muy útiles	***Very useful words***
de vez en cuando	*from time to time*
a veces	*sometimes*
a menudo	*often*
normalmente	*normally*
siempre	*always*
este, esta, estos, estas	*this, these*

Estrategia

Past, present or future?

Future tense verbs are easy to spot, because they are made up of three parts: **1** part of the verb **ir** (to go), **2** the word **a**, **3** an infinitive. For example:
Vamos a jugar al tenis. *We are going to play tennis.*

To tell whether a verb is in the present tense or the preterite, you have to look at the verb ending. For example:
Bail**o** en la discoteca. *I dance at the disco.*
Bail**é** en la discoteca. *I danced at the disco.*

Decide which tense each of the following verbs is in. Then translate the sentences.

- Salgo con mis amigos.
- Vas a ir al cine.
- Fui a Cuba.
- Tomé el sol.
- Escuchamos música.
- Jugué al fútbol.
- Va a ver la televisión.
- Como patatas fritas.

7 La ciudad

- Saying what there is to see and do in Barcelon
- Justifying your opinions of a place

escuchar 1 **Escucha y repite.**

¿Qué hay en Barcelona?

a

el monumento a Colón

b

el Camp Nou

c

el museo Picasso

d

el acuario

e

el Tibidabo

f

el cine IMAX

g

la torre Agbar

h

la Villa Olímpica

i

la Sagrada Familia

j

la plaza de Cataluña

k

la playa de la Barceloneta y el mar

l

las Ramblas

escuchar 2 **¿Adónde van? Escucha y escribe la letra del ejercicio 1 y la razón en inglés. (1–8)**

Ejemplo: **1** d – likes watching sharks

¿Adónde vas?

Voy al/a la …

♥ Me gusta	ver películas
♥♥ Me gusta mucho	ver partidos de fútbol
♥♥♥ Me encanta	ver tiburones
	mirar pinturas
	tomar el sol
	ir de compras
	sacar fotos
	montar en las atracciones del parque

3 Con tu compañero/a, pregunta y contesta.

● ¿Adónde vas?
■ Voy al Camp Nou. Me encanta ver partidos de fútbol.

4 Escucha y elige la frase correcta. (1–5)

Ejemplo: **1** c

a Barcelona es menos grande que Madrid.
b Es una ciudad industrial pero también es antigua.
c Es una ciudad histórica.
d Es menos turística que Benidorm.
e Es la ciudad más bonita de España.

5 Lee los textos y contesta a las preguntas para cada persona.

1 ¿Le gusta Barcelona?
2 ¿Por qué?
3 ¿Qué le gusta hacer en Barcelona?

> me encanta (*I love*)   me gusta (*I like*)
> le encanta (*he/she loves*)   le gusta (*he/she likes*)
>
> Use these phrases with an infinitive or just with a noun:
>
> Me gusta **jugar** al fútbol.   *I like **to play** football.*
> Me gusta el fútbol.   *I like football.*
> Me gustan los museos.   *I like museums.*

miespacio.com

i miespacio *El lugar de los amigos*

Vídeos | Favoritos | Foros | Grupos | Música

¡Hola Barcelona! ¿Cómo estás?

Pregunta del día: "¿Te gusta vivir en Barcelona?"

Juanita Me encanta vivir en Barcelona. Es superguay. :) Hay mucha variedad. Hay barrios históricos como el barrio gótico y barrios modernos y más tranquilos como la Villa Olímpica. Me gusta andar en monopatín por las Ramblas y también sacar fotos de la gente.

Hugo A mí no me gusta nada porque es muy turística. :(Me gusta ver partidos de fútbol en el Camp Nou pero las entradas son muy caras. Prefiero vivir en una ciudad menos turística y menos importante.

barrios = *districts*
gente = *people*

6 Describe tu ciudad.

Me gusta vivir en ... porque ...
Es más/menos ... que ...
Me encanta ... / Me encantan ...
También me gusta ... / También me gustan ...

2 De compras en Barcelona

escuchar 1 Escucha y escribe las letras en el orden correcto.

Ejemplo: h, c, …

una panadería

una cafetería

una carnicería

una pastelería

una joyería

una zapatería

una librería

una tienda de música

una tienda de ropa

un supermercado

escuchar 2 Escucha y escribe la letra correcta. Luego escucha y comprueba tus respuestas. (1–10)

Ejemplo: **1** b

¿Dónde se puede(n) comprar …?

a pasteles

b carne

c pan

d joyas

e zapatos

f libros

g CDs

h un café

i ropa

j comida

hablar 3 Con tu compañero/a, pregunta y contesta sobre los artículos del ejercicio 2.

● ¿Dónde se pueden comprar pasteles?
■ Se pueden comprar pasteles en una pastelería.

Gramática

Singular	¿Dónde **se puede** comprar pan? *Where can you buy bread?*
Plural	¿Dónde **se pueden** comprar pasteles? *Where can you buy cakes?*

Para saber más página 134; ej. 17

Lee los textos y elige los dibujos correctos.

De compras en Barcelona

Elisa

Ayer fui de compras con mi hermana. Lo pasé fenomenal. Primero fui a Zara y luego a Mango, mis tiendas favoritas, y compré unos vaqueros muy bonitos y unas botas negras.

Después fuimos al supermercado y compramos pan, carne y pasteles para la cena. Mañana quiero ir a la Fnac, una tienda de música y videojuegos, y voy a comprar unos CDs.

Pepita

Odio ir de compras. No me gusta nada, pero la semana pasada fui al Corte Inglés. Allí se pueden comprar muchas cosas. Compré unas zapatillas de deporte muy caras y unos vaqueros muy baratos. Compré una sudadera y una gorra también. ¡Lo pasé fatal! Ahora voy a escuchar música …

a

b

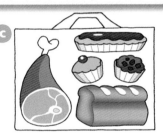
c

Escucha. Copia y rellena la tabla.

Nombre	Tienda	Artículo(s)	Más información
Isabel	zapatería	zapatos	Camper …
Javier			
Natalia			
Miguel			
José			

Copia y completa el texto con las palabras del cuadro.

Ayer **(1)** fui de compras por Barcelona con mi hermano.
(2) _____ fui a la Boquería – el mercado en las Ramblas
– donde **(3)** _____ pan y carne para la cena. Luego fui a una joyería **(4)** _____ compré un regalo muy bonito para mi novia.

Después, con mi hermano, **(5)** _____ a una cafetería cerca de la Boquería donde **(6)** _____ café y comimos **(7)** _____ muy ricos. **(8)** _____ mucho ir de compras en Barcelona. Nunca es aburrido.

primero
~~fui~~
me gusta
bebimos
donde
fuimos
compré
pasteles

regalo = *present*
novia = *girlfriend*

3 ¿Dónde está?

● Asking for and giving directions
● Using **estar** to describe where something is

escuchar 1 Escucha y repite las direcciones.

① Sigue todo recto.

②  Dobla a la derecha.

③ Dobla a la izquierda.

④ Cruza la plaza.

⑤ Toma la segunda calle a la derecha.

⑥ Toma la segunda calle a la izquierda.

⑦  Está al final de la calle.

⑧ Está a la derecha.

⑨ Está a la izquierda.

⑩ Está aquí.

escuchar 2 Escucha y escribe el lugar y la dirección. (1–10)

Ejemplo: **1** e – straight on

¿Dónde está el/la …?

¿Dónde están los/las …?

a
el monumento a Colón

b
el Camp Nou

c
el museo Picasso

d
el acuario

e
el cine IMAX

f
la torre Agbar

g
la Villa Olímpica

h
la plaza de Cataluña

i
la playa de la Barceloneta

j
las Ramblas

Gramática

estar

estoy	I am
estás	you (sing.) are
está	he/she/it is
estamos	we are
estáis	you (plural) are
están	they are

Like **ser**, **estar** means 'to be'. **Ser** describes permanent states.
Estar describes position and temporary conditions.

Barcelona **es** bonita. — Barcelona is nice.
¿Dónde **está** el museo Picasso? — Where is the Picasso Museum?
Estoy bien. — I am well.

Para saber más   página 131; ej. 8

3 Escucha los diálogos y mira el mapa de Barcelona. ¿Adónde van? Escribe la letra correcta. (1–6)

Ejemplo: **1** g

4 Con tu compañero/a, pregunta y contesta.

● Perdón, ¿dónde está el cine IMAX, por favor?

■ A ver … sigue todo recto. Toma la segunda calle a la derecha. Al final de la calle dobla a la derecha y sigue todo recto.

> Use these expressions to give yourself time to think while speaking Spanish.
>
> A ver …
> Bueno …
> Pues …

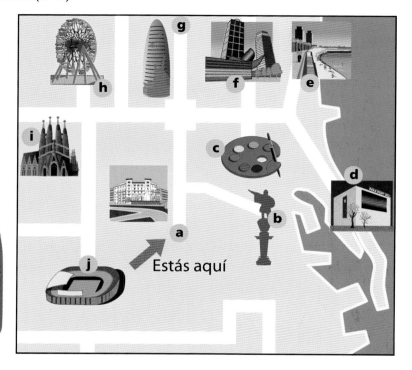

Estás aquí

5 Escribe cinco diálogos sobre el mapa. Utiliza el diálogo del ejercicio 4 como modelo.

6 Escucha y completa la canción con palabras del cuadro. (1–6)

por favor	está	también
A ver	mira	Ah, sí, sí, sí

Mini-test

I can

● say what there is to see and do in Barcelona
● understand types of shop and what you can buy there
● give directions
● use **a ver** and **bueno** to win time while speaking
G use comparative and superlative adjectives
G use **estar** to talk about position

♥ *Barcelona*

Barcelona te quiero,
Todo aquí es bueno …
Barcelona te quiero,
Todo aquí es bueno …

¿Dónde está el museo Picasso?
(1) ~~~ … sigue todo recto.
¿El cine IMAX, **(2)** ~~~?
Al final de la calle, señor.

♥ *Barcelona*

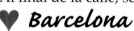

¿Dónde **(3)** ~~~ la Sagrada Familia?
A la izquierda y cruza la plaza.
La playa de la Barceloneta – aquí está.
Y **(4)** ~~~, ¡hay una fiesta!

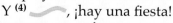

♥ *Barcelona*

¿Te gusta la Villa Olímpica?
Es bonita pero **(5)** ~~~ turística.
¿El Camp Nou está por aquí?
¿La casa del Barça? **(6)** ~~~

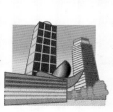

♥ *Barcelona*

4 Soy turista en Barcelona

 1 Escucha y lee. Escribe las letras en la columna correcta de la tabla.

Pasado	Presente	Futuro
a		

Remember how to spot different tenses:

Past	Present	Future
fui	voy	voy a ir
tomé	tomo	voy a tomar
comí	como	voy a comer

Barcelona

a Ayer por la tarde fui a un restaurante.

b Anteayer fui a la playa de la Barceloneta.

c Mañana por la tarde voy a ir al Tibidabo.

d Descansé un poco, tomé el sol y jugué al voleibol.

e Voy a comprar unas camisetas y unos vaqueros.

f Lo pasé fenomenal.

g Hoy voy al acuario y después al cine IMAX.

h Estoy en Barcelona y es genial.

i Pasado mañana voy a ir de compras.

j Comí paella y bebí limonada.

José

ÍÑIGO PONCE

C/ GATO VERDE, 7

31007 VITORIA

ESPAÑA

anteayer	ayer	hoy	mañana	pasado mañana
the day before yesterday	*yesterday*	*today*	*tomorrow*	*the day after tomorrow*

 2 Escribe las frases del ejercicio 1 en un orden lógico.

Ejemplo: Estoy en Barcelona y es genial. ...

3 **Sigue las rayas y di las frases.** *Follow the lines and say the sentences.*

Ejemplo: Anteayer fui al restaurante.

anteayer
ayer
hoy
mañana
pasado mañana

4 **Escucha y lee.**

a
¡Hola! ¿Qué tal? Me llamo Javier. Soy mexicano.

Me encanta Barcelona. Es una ciudad guay. Ayer visité muchos monumentos: la Sagrada Familia, unas iglesias, las casas de Gaudí y el monumento a Colón. Saqué muchas fotos. Por la noche fui a la discoteca y lo pasé genial. Bailé y hablé con muchas personas interesantes.

Hoy quiero ir al museo Picasso porque me gusta pintar y Picasso es mi pintor favorito. Mañana por la tarde voy a ver un partido de fútbol del Barça en el Camp Nou. Me gusta mucho el fútbol. Va a ser fenomenal. Creo que el Barça va a ganar.

b
Me llamo Beverley. Lo siento, pero no me gusta Barcelona. Es una ciudad muy grande y para mí es demasiado turística. Vivo en un pueblo pequeño en Gales y prefiero la tranquilidad.

Además, estoy con mis padres y es muy, muy aburrido. Quiero hablar con mis amigos de mi pueblo. Ayer por la mañana les mandé muchos mensajes.

Ayer por la tarde fui al Tibidabo donde hay un parque de atracciones y me gustó bastante, pero hoy por la mañana fui a la Sagrada Familia y no me gustó nada. Ahora voy a la Villa Olímpica y mañana voy a ir al museo Picasso. Va a ser horrible.

me gustó = *I liked it*
no me gustó = *I didn't like it*

5 **¿Es Javier o Beverley? Escribe J o B.**

Ejemplo: **1** B

Who …
1 doesn't like Barcelona?
2 took a lot of photos?
3 went dancing?
4 is excited about going to the Picasso Museum?
5 has been sending lots of messages?
6 went to the Tibidabo?

6 **Con tu compañero/a, pregunta y contesta por Javier y Beverley.**

- ¿Adónde fuiste ayer?
- ¿Cómo fue?
- ¿Qué haces hoy?
- ¿Qué vas a hacer mañana?

5 Barcelona en tus sueños

 Escucha y lee.

Érase una vez una niña llamada Beverley. Una noche vino un ángel …

1 Beverley, no te gusta Barcelona, ¿verdad? Prefieres las montañas negras de Gales, pero Barcelona es bonita también.

2 Vamos a volar. Uno, dos, tres … Primero vamos al acuario. A ver, todo recto, luego a la derecha, ahora a la izquierda … Y aquí está.

3 Mira, Beverley, los tiburones. Me encanta el acuario. ¿Te gusta, Beverley?

Sí, Ángel, me gusta mucho … No hay tiburones en Gales.

4 ¿Te gusta nadar, Beverley?

Ah sí, me encanta.

Muy bien, vamos a la playa entonces. Todo recto, luego a la izquierda. Mira, el mar.

¡Qué hermoso! ¡Qué bonito es!

5 Y mañana vas al museo Picasso …

¡Oh no! Va a ser horrible … ¡A-bu-rri-do!

No, Beverley, el museo Picasso es fantástico. Es un museo mágico.

6 Por favor, Beverley, Barcelona es una ciudad muy bonita. Disfruta.

Ahora duerme, buenas noches …

Al día siguiente …

7 Papi, mami, ayer por la noche soñé una cosa rarísima …

¡Oh Beverley, por favor! No empieces, no seas negativa …

8 ¿Qué va a hacer hoy en Barcelona, señorita?

Un montón de cosas. Barcelona es la ciudad bonita del mundo. Primero voy al acuario y lueg playa. Después voy al museo Picasso, es mági

… Y colorín colorado este cuento se ha terminado.

hermoso = *wonderful*
disfruta = *enjoy*
duerme = *sleep*
soñé = *I dreamt*
rarísimo = *very strange*
un montón de cosas = *a heap of thin*

2 Lee el carné de identidad y contesta a las preguntas por Beverley.

1 ¿Cuántos años tienes?
2 ¿Cuál es tu nacionalidad?
3 ¿Qué te gusta hacer?
4 ¿Qué no te gusta hacer?

Nombre	Beverley Davies
Edad	14
Nacionalidad	galesa
Me gusta	mandar mensajes
	escuchar música
	pasear al perro
	salir con mis amigos
No me gusta	viajar
	estudiar español

 3 Con tu compañero/a, lee en voz alta el cómic de Beverley (página 104).

 4 Lee otra vez y busca estas frases en el cómic.

Ejemplo: **1** Érase una vez …

1 Once upon a time …
2 one night
3 We are going to fly.
4 Let's see, straight on, then to the right, now to the left …
5 Look – the sea.
6 Now sleep.
7 What are you going to do today in Barcelona?
8 It's the most beautiful city in the world.

 5 Inventa la identidad de una persona que va a visitar una ciudad con Ángel.

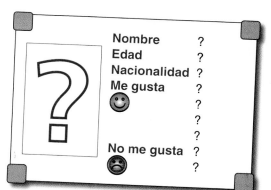

Nombre	?
Edad	?
Nacionalidad	?
Me gusta	?
	?
	?
	?
No me gusta	?
	?

 6 Escribe la historia de Ángel y tu personaje.

Érase una vez un niño llamado …/una niña llamada …
Una noche vino un ángel.
¿No te gusta …? Prefieres …
Vamos a volar.
Primero vamos a … A ver …

Mira … ¿Te gusta?
Y mañana vas a …
Disfruta.
Ahora duerme, buenas noches.
… y colorín colorado este cuento se ha terminado.

Resumen

Unidad 1

I can

- ask and say what there is to see and do in Barcelona

¿Qué hay en Barcelona?
Hay muchas cosas: el acuario, el cine IMAX …

- say where I'm going and why

Voy al Camp Nou. Me encanta ver partidos de fútb

- describe my home town

Birmingham es una ciudad internacional.
Hay barrios modernos.

- say whether I like living there and why

Me encanta vivir en Glasgow porque hay
   museos interesantes.

- **G** use comparative and superlative adjectives

Barcelona es **más turística** que Benidorm.
Es **la** ciudad **más bonita** de España.

Unidad 2

I can

- name different types of shop

una panadería, una zapatería, una librería, …

- ask and say what can be bought there

¿Dónde se puede comprar pan?
Se pueden comprar pasteles en la pastelería.

- read a description of a shopping expedition

Ayer fui de compras y compré muchas cosas.
   Primero fui a …

Unidad 3

I can

- ask for directions

¿Dónde está el monumento a Colón?
¿Dónde están las Ramblas?

- give directions

Sigue todo recto. Cruza la plaza.
   Está al final de la calle.

- use expressions to win time while speaking

A ver … Bueno … Pues …

- **G** use the present tense of **estar** (to be)

estoy, estás, está, estamos, estáis, están

Unidad 4

I can

- describe a holiday in Barcelona

Estoy en Barcelona y es genial. Anteayer fui a la pla
   Ayer por la tarde fui a un restaurante …

- use time expressions

anteayer, ayer, hoy, mañana, pasado mañana

- **G** use past, present and future tenses together

Ayer **descansé** un poco. Hoy **voy** al acuario.
   Mañana **voy a ir** al Tibidabo.

Unidad 5

I can

- read a story set in Barcelona

Érase una vez una niña llamada Beverley.
   Una noche vino un ángel …

- write a story about an invented character

Érase una vez un niño llamado Sean. Un día …

Prepárate

1 Escucha a Paolo y a Mariana. Escribe las letras en la columna correcta de la tabla.

	Ayer	Hoy	Mañana
Paolo	i, ...		
Mariana			

2 Con tu compañero/a, haz cinco diálogos.

● ¿Dónde está la Villa Olímpica?
■ Cruza la plaza y toma la segunda calle a la derecha.

3 Copia las frases con el verbo correcto.

1 Ayer **fui / voy** a la Sagrada Familia con mis padres.
2 Anteayer **vamos / fuimos** al museo Picasso. Fue genial.
3 Hoy **fui / voy** al Camp Nou. Voy a ver un partido de fútbol.
4 Mañana **fui / voy** a comer en un restaurante en las Ramblas.
5 Pasado mañana **fui / voy** a tomar el sol en la playa de la Barceloneta.

4 Escribe frases por Paolo y Mariana del ejercicio 1.

Ejemplo: Ayer visité las Ramblas, …

escuchar 1 Escucha y lee.

Personajes importantes de la historia española

Trajano nació el 18 de septiembre de 53 y murió el 9 de agosto de 117. El emperador romano nació en la ciudad de Itálica en España. Hoy en día la ciudad se llama Santiponce. Está cerca de Sevilla.

Abderramán III nació el 7 de enero de 891 y murió en Córdoba en el año 961. Primero fue Emir de Córdoba y luego Califa. Abderramán III convirtió Córdoba en el centro de un nuevo imperio musulmán en Occidente y en la principal ciudad de Europa.

Isabel la Católica nació el 22 de abril de 1451 y murió el 26 de noviembre de 1504. Hija del rey Juan II de Castilla, Isabel fue reina de Castilla y León desde 1474 hasta 1504. Isabel hizo de la defensa de la fe católica un motivo principal de su reinado.

El Rey Don Juan Carlos I es el actual rey de España. Nació en Roma, Italia, el 5 de enero de 1938. Fue proclamado rey el 22 de noviembre de 1975. Restableció la democracia después de la dictadura de Francisco Franco. Vive en Madrid en la Casa Real con la Reina Doña Sofía, su mujer.

leer 2 Lee el texto. Copia y rellena la tabla.

Name	Birth	Death
Trajano	18/9/53	

> Take your time with dates. Listen for the thousands first, then the hundreds …
>
> 1504 mil quinientos cuatro
> 1975 mil novecientos setenta y cinco

leer 3 Busca estas frases en español en el texto.

1 a new Muslim empire
2 nowadays
3 reign
4 the Roman emperor

5 he re-established democracy
6 he converted
7 he was proclaimed king
8 the defence of the Catholic faith

4 Escucha estos trabalenguas y emparéjalos con los dibujos correctos. (1–5)

Listen to these tongue-twisters and match them to the correct pictures.

1 Pedro Pablo Pérez Pereira, pobre pintor portugués, pinta pinturas por poca plata, para pasar por París.

2 En tres tristes trastos de trigo, Tres tristes tigres comían trigo. Comían trigo tres tristes tigres, En tres tristes trastos de trigo.

3 Pepe Pecas pica papas con un pico, Con un pico pica papas Pepe Pecas.

4 Cuando cuentes cuentos, cuenta cuántos cuentos cuentas, cuando cuentos cuentes.

5 El perro de San Roque no tiene rabo porque Ramón Ramírez se lo ha robado.

plata =	*money*
triste =	*sad*
trasto =	*bowl*
trigo =	*wheat*
papas =	*potatoes*
pico =	*pick*
contar =	*to tell/count*
cuento =	*story*
rabo =	*tail*
ha robado =	*(he) has stolen*

a **b** **c** **d** **e**

5 Con tu compañero/a, repite y traduce los trabalenguas al inglés.

6 Empareja los proverbios españoles con el inglés.

1 Perro ladrador poco mordedor.
2 Más vale pájaro en mano que cien volando.
3 A caballo regalado no le mires el diente.
4 El que ríe el último, ríe mejor.

a *A bird in the hand is worth two in the bush.*
b *Don't look a gift horse in the mouth.*
c *He who laughs last laughs longest.*
d *His bark is worse than his bite!*

escuchar 1 Escucha y lee.

hablar 2 Con tu compañero/a, lee en voz alta la historia de Patricia y Diego.

1

> P – Me interesa mucho el arte y me encanta la arquitectura de Gaudí pero nunca fui al parque Güell. ¿Dónde está exactamente?

2

> D – A ver, ¿ves la montaña? Desde el metro vamos todo recto, luego a la izquierda y está al final de la calle.

3

> P – Mira, Diego, este dragón es precioso. Me encantan estos colores. Estamos en un mundo mágico …

4

> P – ¿Sabes que la arquitectura de Gaudí es modernista? Él siempre utiliza curvas y formas contorneadas. Me encantan sus mosaicos de cerámica. ¡Todo es impresionante!

5

> P – ¿Qué pasa, Diego? ¿No te gusta el parque Güell?
> D – Pues, no Patricia, no me gusta mucho. Creo que no es mi estilo, las esculturas son aburridas.

6

> P – Diego, no pasa nada. No estamos de acuerdo pero te quiero de todas maneras.

no pasa nada =	*it doesn't matter*
estar de acuerdo =	*to agree*
de todas maneras =	*anyway*

ZONA CULTURA

Antoni Gaudí

Antoni Gaudí (1852–1926) fue arquitecto. Estudió en Barcelona.

Utilizó la naturaleza, elementos medievales e influencias orientales en su arquitectura modernista.

Su obra más famosa es la Sagrada Familia. Es el monumento más visitado de España.

Casa de la Pedrera

 leer

3 Busca estas palabras en la historia de Patricia y Diego.

1 art	**3** architecture	**5** modernist	**7** style
2 mosaics	**4** curves	**6** sculptures	**8** twisted forms

 leer

4 Empareja las frases que significan lo mismo.

Ejemplo: **a** más bonito = **i** menos feo

a más bonito   **f** más pequeño

b más histórico   **g** menos moderno

c menos grande   **h** más interesante

d más feo   **i** menos feo

e menos aburrido   **j** menos bonito

 leer

5 Haz una lista de las ciudades en España, desde la más grande hasta la más pequeña.
Make a list of Spanish cities from the largest to the smallest.

Sevilla es más grande que Benidorm.
Córdoba es menos grande que Sevilla.
Gijón es más grande que Benidorm.
Barcelona es más grande que Sevilla.
Madrid es más grande que Barcelona.
Gijón es menos grande que Córdoba.

 escribir

6 Escribe seis frases sobre el Reino Unido, utilizando las frases del ejercicio 5 como modelo.

Palabras

En la ciudad	In the city
¿Qué hay en Barcelona?	What is there in Barcelona?
En Barcelona hay muchas cosas: el acuario, el cine IMAX ...	In Barcelona there are many things: the aquarium, the IMAX cinema...
¿Adónde vas?	Where are you going (to)?
Voy ...	I'm going ...
al acuario	to the aquarium
al Camp Nou	to the Camp Nou (football) stadium
al cine IMAX	to the IMAX cinema
al monumento a Colón	to the Columbus Monument
al museo Picasso	to the Picasso Museum
al Tibidabo	to the Tibidabo funfair
a la playa de la Barceloneta y el mar	to Barceloneta beach and the sea
a la plaza de Cataluña	to the Plaza Cataluña
a la Sagrada Familia	to the Sagrada Familia church
a la torre Agbar	to the Agbar Tower
a la Villa Olímpica	to the Olympic Village
a las Ramblas	to the Ramblas
Me gusta Barcelona porque ...	I like Barcelona because ...
me encanta ...	I love ...
me gusta mucho ...	I really like ...
ir de compras	going shopping
mirar pinturas	looking at paintings
montar en las atracciones del parque	going on the rides at the funfair
sacar fotos	taking photos
tomar el sol	sunbathing
ver partidos de fútbol	watching football matches
ver películas	watching films
ver tiburones	watching sharks
Le gusta (mucho) ...	He/She (really) likes ...
Le encanta ...	He/She loves ...

De compras	Shopping
¿Dónde se puede comprar ...?	Where can you buy ...?
carne	meat
comida	food
pan	bread
ropa	clothes
un café	a coffee
un regalo	a present
¿Dónde se pueden comprar ...?	Where can you buy ...?
pasteles	cakes
joyas	jewellery
zapatos	shoes
libros	books
CDs	CDs
Se puede(n) comprar ...	You can buy ...
en ...	in ...
un supermercado	a supermarket
una cafetería	a café
una carnicería	a butcher's
una joyería	a jeweller's
una librería	a bookshop
una panadería	a baker's/bread shop
una pastelería	a cake shop
una tienda de música	a music shop
una tienda de ropa	a clothes shop
una zapatería	a shoe shop

Las direcciones	Directions
Perdón ...	Excuse me ...
¿Dónde está el museo Picasso?	Where is the Picasso Museum?
¿Dónde están las Ramblas?	Where are the Ramblas?
A ver ...	Let's see ...
Bueno ...	Well ...
Pues ...	Well ...
luego	then

Sigue todo recto.	*Go straight on.*
Dobla a la derecha.	*Turn right.*
Dobla a la izquierda.	*Turn left.*
Cruza la plaza.	*Cross the square.*
Toma la segunda calle a la derecha.	*Take the second (street) on the right.*
Toma la segunda calle a la izquierda.	*Take the second (street) on the left.*
(Está) al final de la calle.	*(It's) at the end of the street.*
Está a la derecha.	*It's on the right.*
Está a la izquierda.	*It's on the left.*
Está aquí.	*It's here.*

Soy turista …	***I'm a tourist …***
Hoy …	*Today …*
Estoy en Barcelona.	*I'm in Barcelona.*
Es genial.	*It's great.*
Anteayer …	*The day before yesterday …*
Ayer por la tarde …	*Yesterday evening …*
fui a la playa	*I went to the beach*
comí paella y bebí limonada	*I ate paella and drank lemonade*
descansé un poco	*I had a little rest*
Lo pasé fenomenal.	*I had a wonderful time.*
Me gustó.	*I liked it.*
No me gustó.	*I didn't like it.*

Mañana …	*Tomorrow …*
Pasado mañana …	*The day after tomorrow …*
voy a ir al Tibidabo	*I'm going to go to the Tibidabo*
voy a ir de compras	*I'm going to go shopping*
voy a comprar unas camisetas	*I'm going to buy some T-shirts*

Palabras muy útiles	***Very useful words***
a (al)	*to (to the)*
hay	*there is/there are*
¿dónde?	*where?*
¿adónde?	*(to) where?*
en	*in, at*
hoy	*today*
ayer	*yesterday*
anteayer	*the day before yesterday*
mañana	*tomorrow*

Estrategia

The gender of nouns

You can often work out whether a noun is masculine or feminine by looking at the ending of the word:
- Most nouns ending in **-o**, **-or** and **-ón** are masculine.
- Most nouns ending in **-a**, **-dad** and **-ción** are feminine.

But be careful! There are exceptions, for example:
el problema   **la** foto

To check, use a dictionary: look for the abbreviations *nm* (masculine noun) and *nf* (feminine noun).

Can you work out the gender of these nouns from Module 6 without using a dictionary?

ciudad	supermercado	pastelería
pintor	tiburón	canción

Te toca a ti A

 1 **Look at the information. Write six sentences.**

Ejemplo: Penélope Cruz es más alta que Salma Hayek.

Antonio Banderas
1,75m   10/8/1960

Gael García Bernal
1,68m   30/11/1978

Penélope Cruz
1,64m   28/4/1974

Salma Hayek
1,58m   2/9/1966

Inés Sastre
1,73m   21/11/1973

 2 **Copy out the form and fill it in for yourself.**

Nombre	Paco Torres
Nacionalidad	colombiano
Edad	15
☺	cómics
Actividades	juego al fútbol
Carácter	inteligente y divertido
Pelo	corto y castaño
Ojos	marrones

3 **Write four dialogues.**

Ejemplo: – ¿Qué haces por la mañana, Isabel?
– Me peino, desayuno y voy al instituto.

me despierto	me ducho	
me levanto	me peino	me visto
desayuno	voy al instituto	

Isabel

Natalia

Roberto

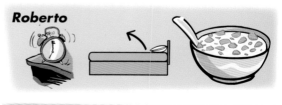

Omar

leer

1 *Choose the correct words.*

Ejemplo: El mejor amigo de Pepe se llama Antonio.

El mejor **amiga** / **amigo** de Pepe se llama Antonio. **Tiene** / **Tengo** dieciocho años.
Es **alto** / **alta**. Tiene **el pelo** / **los ojos** corto y castaño. **Tengo** / **Tiene** los ojos
marrones. Es divertido **y** / **pero** generoso. **Te gusta** / **Le gusta** leer y hacer deporte.

leer

2 *Who is it? Write the correct name. (There is one picture too many.)*

www.mejores–amigos.es

Amigos para siempre – ¡tenemos tanto en común!

Silvia　**Carlos**

Tico　**Lola**

1
Mi mejor amigo es bastante bajo. Es muy inteligente
y no es perezoso. Tiene el pelo pelirrojo y rizado.
Tiene los ojos marrones. Le gusta hacer deporte.

2
Mi mejor amiga es muy guapa y muy delgada. Es
seria y tranquila. Tiene el pelo castaño y largo y los
ojos negros. Le gusta leer y escuchar música.

3
Mi mejor amigo es alto. Es inteligente y bastante
generoso, pero no es hablador. Tiene el pelo castaño
y corto y tiene los ojos marrones. Le gustan los
cómics y los videojuegos pero también le gusta
tomar el sol.

escribir

3 *Write the website text describing these people.*

Ejemplo: **a** Mi mejor amigo es bastante alto. …

SILENCIO POR FAVOR

escribir

1 Write the questions out correctly and underline the infinitives.
Then translate them into English.

Ejemplo: **1** ¿Quieres <u>ir</u> al estadio? – Do you want to go to the stadium?

1 ir ¿Quieres estadio? al

2 discoteca? a ¿Quieres ir la

3 a la bolera? ir ¿Quieres

4 película? ¿Quieres una ver

5 salir? ¿Quieres

6 ¿Quieres fútbol? al jugar

7 chatear internet? ¿Quieres por

8 de ¿Quieres compras? ir

 leer

2 Where are they going to meet? Match up the two halves of the
notes and then translate them into English.

Ejemplo: **1** d Quedamos en la bolera. – Let's meet in the bowling alley.

1 Quedamos en la b

2 Quedamos en tu ca

3 Quedamos detrás del centro comer

4 Quedamos delante del es

5 Quedamos en el salón re

6 Quedamos delante de la dis

a cial

b creativo

c coteca

d olera

e tadio

f sa

 leer

3 Write out the words in the wordsnakes with the correct punctuation.
Then match the excuses to the pictures.

Ejemplo: **1** Lo siento, no puedo. Tengo que leer mi perro. – b

1 losientonopuedotengoqueleermiperro

2 losientonopuedotengoquecomermidiccionario

3 losientonopuedotengoquepasearamihermana

4 losientonopuedotengoquelavarmelospies

5 losientonopuedotengoqueescucharelsol

a
b
c
d
e

1 Choose the correct infinitive. Write out the sentence and then translate it into English.

Ejemplo: **1** Juanita va a ver la nueva película de James Bond.
Juanita is going to see the new James Bond film.

Este fin de semana …

1 Juanita va a **comer** / **ver** la nueva película de James Bond.
2 Sergio va a **mandar** / **escuchar** mensajes a sus amigos.
3 Natalia va a **beber** / **leer** un libro interesante.
4 Jorge va a **escuchar** / **pintar** música.
5 Carmen va a **hacer** / **jugar** deporte.

2 Write five sentences about yourself, using the infinitives you didn't use in exercise 1 and the phrases below.

Ejemplo: Voy a comer …

al voleibol con mi gato   mil hamburguesas   las estrellas   dos litros de limonada   tres sinfonías y dos óperas

3 Read Jaume's text and complete the sentences in English.

Ejemplo: **1** Normally Jaume sends text messages and listens to music.

Normalmente en mi tiempo libre mando mensajes y escucho música. También hago deporte. Me gusta mucho hacer esquí acuático y jugar al voleibol, pero este fin de semana quiero relajarme un poco. Voy a ir al balneario y a la peluquería. Por la noche voy a salir con unos amigos y vamos a ir a la discoteca y al casino.

1 Normally Jaume …
2 He also …
3 Jaume likes to …
4 This weekend he wants to …
5 He is going to go to …
6 In the evening he is going to …

4 Write as if you were Pria Fredericks, using the exercise 3 text as a model.

Normalmente …

 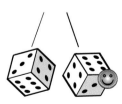

Este fin de semana …

Te toca a ti A

1 **Solve the anagrams. Write out the sentences and match each one to a picture.**

Ejemplo: **1** Lo pasé guay. – c

 a
 b
 c

1 Lo pasé gyua
2 Lo pasé nbie
3 Lo pasé noeenalfm
4 Lo pasé mla
5 Lo pasé aobmb

 d
 e

2 **Write out the questions and answers in pairs.**

Ejemplo: **1** ¿Adónde fuiste de vacaciones?
Fui a Italia.

1 ¿Adónde fuiste de vacaciones?
2 ¿Con quién fuiste?
3 ¿Cómo fuiste?
4 ¿Qué hiciste?
5 ¿Cómo fue?

a Fui a Italia.
b Fui de excursión y visité monumentos.
Por la noche, fuimos a la discoteca.
c Fui con mis amigos.
d Fue guay.
e Fui en avión.

3 **Match up the holidays to the descriptions. (There is one description too many.)**

1
2
3

a Fui a Barcelona.
Fui en barco.
Descansé un poco, tomé el sol y visité monumentos.
Fue genial.

b Fui de vacaciones a Pontevedra.
Fui con mi familia en coche.
Monté en bicicleta y tomé el sol. Fue estupendo.

c Fui a Madrid.
Fui con mis amigos.
Fuimos en coche.
Visité monumentos y saqué fotos. Fue guay.

d Fui de vacaciones a Palma de Mallorca. Fui en avión.
Fui con mi familia y fue muy aburrido.
Fuimos de compras y fuimos a la playa.

escribir 1 Put the words in the wordsnake into three groups.

españamandécochegreciatrenaviónjuguéfuiautocarportugalbailébarcoargentinadescanséescocia

Transporte	Verbos	Países
coche	mandé	España

leer 2 Who is talking: Claudia or Norberto?
Write C or N.

Ejemplo: **1** N

Palma

Normalmente voy a Madrid de vacaciones y voy de compras. Me encanta ir de compras. Mando mensajes a mis amigos todos los días.

El año pasado fui a Francia con mi hermana. Fuimos en coche. Monté a caballo y fui de excursión a la montaña. Fue estupendo. También fui a la torre Eiffel. Lo pasé fenomenal.

Claudia

Normalmente voy a Palma de Mallorca de vacaciones. Voy a la playa, tomo el sol y escucho música. Juego al voleibol un poco y hago natación también. Por la noche voy a la discoteca.

Pero el año pasado fui a Roma con mi padre. Fuimos en avión y luego en autocar. Visité monumentos y museos. Fue un poco aburrido. Lo pasé mal. Prefiero la playa.

Norberto

escribir 3 Copy out the text with the correct verbs.

Ejemplo: … (**1**) Visité monumentos …

El año pasado fui a Grecia de vacaciones. **(1) Visité / Escuché** monumentos y **(2) monté / mandé** mensajes. **(3) Jugué / Tomé** al fútbol y **(4) bailé / monté** en bicicleta también. **(5) Tomé / Mandé** el sol en la playa. Lo pasé bomba. **(6) Fui / Fue** guay.

escribir

1 Match up the word halves and then write a sentence using each word.

Ejemplo: Normalmente como lechuga.

lech   **tos**   **ensa**   **uga**

ales   **cere**

ado

magda   **tadas**   **pes**

hel   **llo**   **po**   **lenas**

lada

cado

 leer

2 Put the pictures in the same order as the dialogue.

Ejemplo: d, …

Camarero	Buenos días, señora. ¿Qué va a tomar?
Señora	De primer plato quiero ensalada.
	De segundo plato quiero paella.
	Y de postre quiero fruta.
Camarero	¿Para beber?
Señora	Agua, por favor.
Camarero	Muy bien, señora.

 leer

3 Match up the dinosaurs with the shopping bags. (There is one bag too many.)

1 Nunca como carne. Soy herbívora. Como fruta y verduras. Hoy en el mercado compré quince lechugas, veinte pepinos y diez kilos de peras.

2 Como plantas pero no me gusta la ensalada: prefiero la fruta. Hoy en el mercado compré cinco kilos de uvas y tres kilos de peras.

3 Como carne, pero también como verduras. Hoy compré un kilo de jamón, cinco lechugas, dos kilos de tomates, diez pepinos y quinientos gramos de queso. Voy a preparar una ensalada griega …

Belén Braquiosaurio

Paco Parasaurolofus

Teresa Tiranosaurio

a

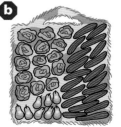
b

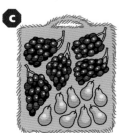
c

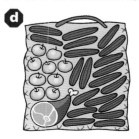
d

1 Match up the sentence halves.

Las horas de comer en España

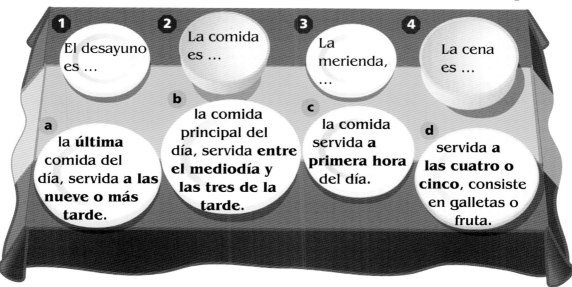

1 El desayuno es …

2 La comida es …

3 La merienda, …

4 La cena es …

a la **última** comida del día, servida **a las nueve o más tarde.**

b la comida principal del día, servida **entre el mediodía y las tres de la tarde.**

c la comida servida a **primera hora del día.**

d servida **a las cuatro o cinco**, consiste en galletas o fruta.

2 Copy out the text and fill in the gaps.

Ejemplo: … el ganador Diego (**1**) comió gusanos …

Diego gana el premio de supervivientes

Para ganar el premio del día, el ganador Diego **(1) comió / comiste** gusanos, moscas, cucarachas y arañas. **(2) Gané / Ganó** una cesta de comida con pollo, pescado, ensalada y fruta.

No **(3) compartimos / compartió** su comida con sus amigos. **(4) Comieron / Comió** todo en su tienda. No **(5) vomité / vomitó**.

supervivientes = *survivors*
cesta = *basket*
tienda = *tent*

3 Translate these jokes into English.

¿Va a tomar una tortilla española o una tortilla francesa?
No importa.
No voy a hablar con ella.

¿No vas a comer los caracoles?
No. Prefiero la comida rápida.

leer

1 Unjumble these items of clothing and then match them to the pictures.

Ejemplo: **1** unas botas – j

1 suna toabs
2 aun simateac
3 nu seeryj
4 nuso qosreuav
5 nu soditve
6 nuso poatzsa
7 nau rroga
8 nua radedusa
9 anu dalfa
10 nuas llaspatiza ed tropede
11 nua taquecha
12 sonu nspetalona

a **g**
b **h**
c **i**
d **j**
e **k**
f **l**

escribir

2 Write eight sentences saying whether or not you like these items of clothing.

Ejemplo: **1** Me gusta este jersey.

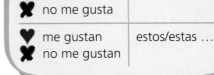

| ♥ me gusta / ✗ no me gusta | este/esta … |
| ♥ me gustan / ✗ no me gustan | estos/estas … |

1    **2** 

3    **4**    **5**

6    **7**    **8**

escribir

3 Copy out the text and fill the gaps with phrases from the box. (There is one phrase too many.)

¡Hola! Me llamo Cintia. Soy chilena. Me gustan
(1) . Me encanta (2) y (3) también.

Normalmente llevo (4) y (5) pero mañana voy a ir de excursión.

Primero voy a montar en bicicleta y luego voy a montar a caballo. Voy a llevar (6) , (7) y (8) .

unos vaqueros   una falda   escuchar música   una camiseta
los videojuegos   leer   los cómics   una sudadera   unas botas

leer

1 Which item is the most expensive? List the items in order, from least expensive to most expensive.

Las botas son menos caras que las zapatillas de deporte.
La falda es más cara que la camiseta.
La camiseta es más cara que la gorra.
Las botas son más caras que la falda.
Las zapatillas de deporte son menos caras que los zapatos.

 escribir

2 Write the opposites of these adjectives.

1 feo   **2** incómodo   **3** caro   **4** anticuado

 escribir

3 Copy out the conversation and fill the gaps with words from the box. (There is one word too many.)

cómoda
cuál
esta
gustan
más
menos
prefiero

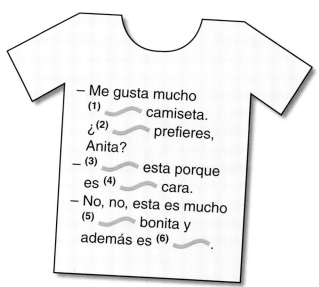

– Me gusta mucho **(1)** _____ camiseta. ¿**(2)** _____ prefieres, Anita?

– **(3)** _____ esta porque es **(4)** _____ cara.

– No, no, esta es mucho **(5)** _____ bonita y además es **(6)** _____.

 escribir

4 Translate these sentences into Spanish.

Ejemplo: **1** Este jersey es el más cómodo.

1 This sweater is the most comfortable.
2 This T-shirt is the cheapest.
3 This dress is the least expensive.
4 This sweatshirt is the least comfortable.
5 These jeans are the nicest.
6 These boots are the most practical.

1 Fill in the missing letters in these time expressions. Then match up the Spanish and the English.

Ejemplo: ayer = yesterday

*y*r
o
*a*a*a
*a*a*o *a*a*a
a**ea*er

the day before yesterday
yesterday
the day after tomorrow
tomorrow
today

 2 Write out the questions and answers.

Ejemplo:
1 ¿Dónde está el museo?
Sigue todo recto y cruza la plaza.

3 Write out the sentences correctly. Are they about the past, present or future?

Ejemplo:
1 Estoy en Barcelona y me encanta el acuario. – present

1

2

3

4

el hospital   el museo   la piscina
la plaza de toros

1 estoyenbarcelonaymeencantaelacuario

2 ayerfuialaplayaporlamañana

3 luegofuiaunrestaurantecomisamigos

4 despuésfuialadiscotecaybailémucho

5 hoyquieroverlatelevisiónencasa

6 mañanavoyahacersurf

7 despuésvoyacomertapasenunba

leer

1 Which adjective in each group is the odd one out? Give a reason for your answer (there may be more than one answer!). Then write a sentence in Spanish using the adjective.

Ejemplo: **1** bonita – It's feminine. – Vivo en una ciudad bonita.

1 a moderno	**b** tranquilo	**c** bonita
2 a histórico	**b** histórica	**c** históricas
3 a moderno	**b** grande	**c** moderna
4 a industrial	**b** importante	**c** grandes
5 a pequeña	**b** bonito	**c** tranquila
6 a feo	**b** turístico	**c** fea

escribir

2 Match up the sentence halves and write out the completed text.

Me encanta vivir en Manchester — animada.

También es — bailar en las discotecas.

Es muy — porque hay monumentos y museos.

Sobre todo me gusta — una ciudad moderna e importante.

leer

3 Read what Antonia says and correct the mistakes in the sentences.

Ejemplo: **1** Antonia es inglesa.

1 Antonia es española.
2 No le gusta Barcelona.
3 Ayer visitó el Camp Nou.
4 No sacó fotos.
5 Fue al casino. Lo pasó fatal.
6 No le gusta cantar.
7 Mañana por la tarde va a ver un partido de fútbol.
8 No le gusta nada el cine.

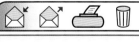

¡Hola! ¿Qué tal?

Soy inglesa. Me llamo Antonia.

Me encanta Barcelona. Es una ciudad guay. Ayer visité unos monumentos y saqué muchas fotos. Por la noche fui a la discoteca y lo pasé genial. Bailé y hablé con muchas personas interesantes.

Hoy quiero ir a la ópera porque me gusta escuchar música. También me gusta cantar.

Mañana por la tarde voy a ver una película en el Cine IMAX. Me gusta mucho ir al cine.

Gramática

Glossary of grammar terms

adjective
a word describing a noun (*divertido* – entertaining)

connective
a joining word (*pero* – but, *porque* – because)

demonstrative adjective
an adjective used to point out a noun (**esta** *camiseta* – **this** T-shirt)

definite article
the word for 'the' (*el/la/los/las*)

infinitive
the dictionary form of a verb, ending in **-ar**, **-er** or **-ir** in Spanish (*escuchar* – to listen, *leer* – to read, *vivir* – to live, *ser* – to be)

indefinite article
the word for 'a' (*un/una*) or 'some' (*unos/unas*)

gender
whether a word is masculine or feminine (*un bocadillo* – m, *una pizza* – f)

noun
a word naming a person or thing (*amigo* – friend)

preposition
a word or phrase showing the relationship of one thing to another (*debajo de* – under) or showing possession (*de* – of, 's)

preterite
the simple past tense, used to refer to an action or event in the past (*salí con mis amigos* – I went out with my friends)

pronoun
a word that stands for a noun (*yo* – I, *tú* – you, *él* – he, *ella* – she)

possessive adjective
an adjective showing who something belongs to (*mi* – my, *tu* – your, *su* – his/her)

qualifier
a word that makes a description more specific (*muy* – very)

reflexive verb
a verb that includes a pronoun referring back to the subject (**me** *ducho* – I shower (myself))

tense
a verb form showing when an action takes place (**voy** *a la piscina* – now/normally: present tense, **fui** *a al piscina* – in the past: preterite, **voy a ir** *a la piscina* – in the future: near future tense)

verb
a word that refers to an action or event (*como* – I eat, *llueve* – it rains); it can also refer to an ongoing state (**es** *guapo* – he **is** good-looking); **regular verbs** follow the patterns of one of the three verb groups (**-ar/-er/-ir**), but **irregular verbs** don't

1 Nouns

1.1 Gender

A noun is a word that names a person or thing. In Spanish all nouns have a gender: masculine or feminine. Nouns ending in **-o** are usually masculine (e.g. **estadio**); nouns ending in **-a** are usually feminine (e.g. **playa**). For other nouns, you need to learn the gender when you learn the word:

el fútbol (masculine)   **la ciudad** (feminine)

1.2 Singular/Plural

The plural is used when referring to more than one of something. The form of the plural depends on the noun's ending:

ends in a vowel	add **-s**	libro**s** *books*
ends in a consonant	add **-es**	móvil**es** *mobile phones*
ends in **-z**	change **z** to **c** and add **-es**	lápi**zces** *pencils*

1.3 The indefinite article ('a/an', 'some')

In Spanish the words for 'a/an' and 'some' change according to the gender of the noun and whether it is singular or plural.

	Singular	Plural
masculine	**un** libro *a book*	**unos** libros *some books*
feminine	**una** mochila *a schoolbag*	**unas** mochilas *some schoolbags*

1.4 The definite article ('the')

The Spanish for 'the' also changes according to the gender of the noun and whether it is singular or plural.

	Singular	Plural
masculine	**el** ordenador *the computer*	**los** ordenadores *the computers*
feminine	**la** ventana *the window*	**las** ventanas *the windows*

2 Pronouns

A pronoun takes the place of a noun.

Jenny → she   the game → it

Spanish has words for 'I', 'you', 'he', 'she', etc., but generally they are not used with verbs: the verb on its own is enough. However, you do need to be able to recognise them.

yo	*I*
tú	*you (singular)*
él	*he*
ella	*she*
nosotros	*we (male)*
nosotras	*we (female)*
vosotros	*you (plural, male)*
vosotras	*you (plural, female)*
ellos	*they (male)*
ellas	*they (female)*

3 Adjectives

3.1 Agreement of adjectives

ending in ...	Singular		Plural	
	masc.	fem.	masc.	fem.
-o or -a	divertido	divertida	divertidos	divertidas
-e	grande	grande	grandes	grandes
consonant*	fácil	fácil	fáciles	fáciles

* Note that **hablador** and other adjectives ending in **-or** have different feminine forms, although they end in a consonant, e.g. **habladora(s)**.

Colours

Colour words are adjectives and generally follow the same patterns as the adjectives above, with a few exceptions. For example, **rosa – rosas** *(pink)* and **naranja – naranjas** *(orange)* change only in the plural.

ending in ...	Singular		Plural	
	masculine	feminine	masculine	feminine
-o or -a	negro	negra	negros	negras
-e	verde	verde	verdes	verdes
consonant	azul	azul	azules	azules

Nationalities

Nationalities are also adjectives. Nationality words ending in **-o/-a** and **-e** follow the patterns above, but those ending in a consonant have different feminine forms, e.g. **escocesa(s)**.

Gramática

ending in ...	Singular	
	masculine	**feminine**
-o or -a	mexican**o**	mexican**a**
-e	estadounidense	estadounidense
consonant	escocés	escoce**sa**

ending in ...	Plural	
	masculine	**feminine**
-o or -a	mexican**os**	mexican**as**
-e	estadounidense**s**	estadounidense**s**
consonant	escoce**ses**	escoce**sas**

3.2 Position of adjectives

In Spanish, most adjectives follow the noun they are describing.

Tiene los ojos **marrones**.   She has **brown** eyes.
Me gustan los chicos **inteligentes**.
    I like **intelligent** boys.

3.3 Comparatives

When you want to compare two things, you use the comparative form of the adjective:

más + adjective + **que** = *more ... than*
menos + adjective + **que** = *less ... than*

The adjective agrees with the noun it describes.

Diego es **más alto que** Cristina.
    *Diego is **taller** (literally: **more tall**) **than** Cristina.*
Madonna es **menos guapa que** Shakira.
    *Madonna is **less pretty than** Shakira.*

Exercise 1
Write out the text, using the correct comparative adjectives.

¿Mis amigos? Pues, Carmen es (1) más seria que María, pero ...

¿Mis amigos? Pues, Carmen es **(1)** *(more serious than)* María, pero es **(2)** *(less generous than)* Patricia. Javier es **(3)** *(taller than)* Diego. Juan es **(4)** *(more attractive than)* Javier. María es **(5)** *(lazier than)* Juan. Patricia es **(6)** *(less talkative than)* Carmen.

3.4 Superlatives

When you want to say 'the biggest', 'the smallest', etc., you use the superlative form of the adjective. It consists of the appropriate definite article + **más/menos** + adjective. The adjective agrees with the noun it describes.

Este vestido es **el más cómodo**.
    *This dress is **the most comfortable**.*
Estas botas son **las menos prácticas**.
    *These boots are **the least practical**.*
Barcelona es **la** ciudad **más bonita** de España.
    *Barcelona is **the most attractive** city in Spain.*

Exercise 2
Rewrite each sentence in the correct order, and then translate it into English.

1 es caro vestido el más este
   – Este vestido es el más caro.
   This dress is the most expensive.
2 más estas son las botas incómodas
3 los vaqueros caros son estos menos
4 zapatos más estos los bonitos son
5 es la chaqueta cómoda menos esta
6 feos más estos los pantalones son
7 corbata anticuada es esta la menos
8 más jersey es el guay este

3.5 Possessive adjectives ('my', etc.)

Possessive adjectives are the words for 'my', 'your', etc. They agree with the noun they describe.

	Singular	Plural
my	mi hermano/a	mi**s** hermano**s**/a**s**
your	tu hermano/a	tu**s** hermano**s**/a**s**
his/her/its	su hermano/a	su**s** hermano**s**/a**s**

3.6 Demonstrative adjectives ('this', 'these')

The word for 'this' and 'these' changes its ending depending on whether the noun it describes is masculine or feminine, singular or plural.

Singular		Plural	
masculine	**feminine**	**masculine**	**feminine**
est**e** vestido	est**a** chaqueta	est**os** zapatos	est**as** botas

Exercise 3

Write out each phrase using the correct form of **este**. Look carefully at the noun endings to see which are singular and which are plural.

1. ～ corbata (f) – *esta corbata*
2. ～ cómics (m)
3. ～ coche (m)
4. ～ camisetas (f)
5. ～ jersey (m)
6. ～ chica (f)
7. ～ fotos (m)
8. ～ patatas fritas (f)
9. ～ tienda (f)
10. ～ pantalones (m)

4 Verbs

4.1 The infinitive

The infinitive is the form of a verb used in a dictionary or wordlist. In Spanish, regular verbs fall into three groups, with infinitives ending in **-ar**, **-er** or **-ir**.

4.2 The present tense

The present tense is used to talk about what usually happens (e.g. *I go to school every day*) or about how things are (e.g. *French lessons are very boring*). In Spanish, it can also be used to talk about what is happening now (e.g. *I am doing my homework*).

(a) regular verbs

	-ar verbs
	hablar – *to speak*
(yo – *I*)	habl**o**
(tú – *you*)	habl**as**
(él/ella – *he/she*)	habl**a**
(nosotros/as – *we*)	habl**amos**
(vosotros/as – *you*)	habl**áis**
(ellos/as – *they*)	habl**an**

	-er verbs	-ir verbs
	comer – *to eat*	**escribir** – *to write*
(yo – *I*)	com**o**	escrib**o**
(tú – *you*)	com**es**	escrib**es**
(él/ella – *he/she*)	com**e**	escrib**e**
(nosotros/as – *we*)	com**emos**	escrib**imos**
(vosotros/as – *you*)	com**éis**	escrib**ís**
(ellos/as – *they*)	com**en**	escrib**en**

(b) stem-changing verbs

Stem-changing verbs are verbs which are usually regular in their endings, but have a vowel change in the 'stem' (the part to which the endings are added) in some forms of the present tense.

	jugar – *to play*	**dormir** – *to sleep*
(yo)	ju**e**go	d**ue**rmo
(tú)	ju**e**gas	d**ue**rmes
(él/ella)	ju**e**ga	d**ue**rme
(nosotros/as)	jugamos	dormimos
(vosotros/as)	jugáis	dormís
(ellos/as)	ju**e**gan	d**ue**rmen

	poder – *to be able, 'can'*	**querer** – *to want*
(yo)	p**ue**do	qu**ie**ro
(tú)	p**ue**des	qu**ie**res
(él/ella)	p**ue**de	qu**ie**re
(nosotros/as)	podemos	queremos
(vosotros/as)	podéis	queréis
(ellos/as)	p**ue**den	qu**ie**ro

Poder and **querer** are usually followed by another verb in the infinitive: see section **4.9**.

Exercise 4

Write out each sentence with the correct form of **poder** or **querer**. Then translate the sentences into English.

1. ～ ir a la discoteca. *(we want)*
   – *Queremos ir a la discoteca.*
   We want to go to the disco.
2. No ～ ordenar mi dormitorio. *(I want)*
3. ～ hacer sus deberes mañana. *(he can)*
4. No ～ pasear al perro. *(I can)*
5. ～ ver un partido de fútbol. *(they want)*
6. ～ ver una película. *(you can – plural)*
7. ～ jugar al fútbol. *(she wants)*
8. ¿ ～ ir de compras? *(you want – singular)*

(c) reflexive verbs

Reflexive verbs describe an action which you do to yourself. To show this, they include a pronoun which means 'myself', 'yourself', etc., although this pronoun is not always translated, e.g. **me** ducho – *I shower* (literally: *I shower **myself***).

Reflexive verbs are generally regular in their endings, but some are stem-changing verbs.

	ducharse – *to shower*	**despertarse** – *to wake up* (stem-changing)
(yo)	**me** ducho	**me** desp**ie**rto
(tú)	**te** duchas	**te** desp**ie**rtas
(él/ella)	**se** ducha	**se** desp**ie**rta
(nosotros/as)	**nos** duchamos	**nos** despertamos
(vosotros/as)	**os** ducháis	**os** despertáis
(ellos/as)	**se** duchan	**se** desp**ie**rtan

Exercise 5

Match the sentence halves, write out the sentences and then translate them into English.

1 Normalmente me
2 Mi madre se
3 Desayunamos en la cocina y luego nos
4 Mis hermanos se
5 ¿Te
6 Por la tarde cenáis y os

peinan y luego van al instituto.
acostáis muy tarde.
despierto muy temprano.
lavamos los dientes.
duchas por la mañana?
levanta a las siete.

(d) irregular verbs

Some verbs are not regular in the present tense: they don't follow the usual patterns for **-ar**, **-er** or **-ir** verbs. Some of the most useful irregular verbs are given below.

	hacer – *to do*	**salir** – *to go out*
(yo)	ha**g**o	sal**g**o
(tú)	haces	sales
(él/ella)	hace	sale
(nosotros/as)	hacemos	salimos
(vosotros/as)	hacéis	salís
(ellos/as)	hacen	salen

	tener – *to have* (also stem-changing)	**ir** – *to go*
(yo)	**tengo**	**voy**
(tú)	**tie**nes	**vas**
(él/ella)	**tie**ne	**va**
(nosotros/as)	tenemos	**vamos**
(vosotros/as)	tenéis	**vais**
(ellos/as)	**tie**nen	**van**

	ser – *to be*	**estar** – *to be*
(yo)	**soy**	est**oy**
(tú)	**eres**	est**ás**
(él/ella)	**es**	est**á**
(nosotros/as)	**somos**	estamos
(vosotros/as)	**sois**	estáis
(ellos/as)	**son**	est**án**

Exercise 6

tener or **ser**? Choose the correct verb to complete each sentence. Write out the sentences and translate them into English.

1 Mi amigo **es / tiene** quince años.
2 Mis hermanas **son / tienen** divertidas.
3 Penélope Cruz **es / tiene** muy baja.
4 Soy guapo. **Soy / Tengo** el pelo rubio.
5 ¿**Eres / Tienes** hermanos, Patricia?
6 Tengo doce años y **soy / tengo** habladora.
7 Los chicos **son / tienen** los ojos marrones.
8 Mi madre y yo **somos / tenemos** un poco perezosos.

tener que

The verb **tener** is also used in the expression **tener que**, which means 'to have to'. **Tener que** is followed by another verb in the infinitive.

Tiene que ordenar su dormitorio.
*He **has to tidy** his room.*

Exercise 7

Write out each sentence using **tengo** or **tengo que** and then translate it into English.

1 ～ ordenar mi dormitorio.
2 ～ un perro y un gato.
3 Lo siento, no ～ tiempo.
4 No ～ pasear al perro.
5 ～ trece años.
6 ～ ir de compras.

ser/estar

In Spanish there are two verbs meaning *to be*: **ser** and **estar**.

Ser is used to refer to ongoing or permanent states: **eres** alto – *you're tall*, **es** negro – *it's black*, ¿Cómo **eres**? – *What are you like?*

It is also used for telling the time:

¿Qué hora **es**? **Son** las cuatro.
   What time is it? It's 4 o'clock.

Estar is used to refer to position and temporary conditions:

¿Dónde **está**?   *Where is it?*
¿Cómo **estás**?   *How are you?*

Exercise 8
ser or **estar**? Are the verbs used the correct ones? Find the four other sentences that use the wrong verb and correct them.

1 Barcelona es en la costa. – *Barcelona está en la costa.*
2 Es una ciudad muy importante.
3 Los vaqueros negros son muy bonitos.
4 Son al final de la calle.
5 ¡Estamos en Sevilla y es genial!
6 Soy escocesa.
7 Están las dos y diez.
8 Mi amiga es muy inteligente.
9 Es aquí.
10 Mi piso está moderno.

4.3   The near future tense
The near future tense is used to talk about what you are 'going to' do. It is formed with the present-tense form of **ir** + **a** + a verb in the infinitive.
(See section **4.2(d)** for the present tense of **ir**.)

Mañana **voy a jugar** al fútbol.
   Tomorrow I'm going to play football.
Vamos a ver una película.
   We're going to see a film.
¿Qué **vas a hacer**?   *What are you going to do?*

Exercise 9
Write out each sentence in the correct order, and then translate it into English.

1 ver película voy a una
   – *Voy a ver una película.*
   I'm going to watch a film.
2 televisión a ver la van
3 ¿ ? hacer qué a vas
4 va al jugar futbolín a
5 escuchar va a música
6 voy a de fútbol ver un partido
7 van a España ir a
8 y voy a playa ir a la el sol tomar voy a
9 a amigos voy salir con mis
10 voy a discoteca en una bailar

4.4   The preterite
The preterite (or 'simple past tense') is used to talk about events in the past that are now finished.

Ayer **fui** de excursión.   *Yesterday I went on a trip.*
Saqué fotos.   *I took photos.*
Fue guay.   *It was great.*

(a) regular verbs

	-ar verbs	
	visitar – to visit	
(yo)	visit**é**	I visited
(tú)	visit**aste**	you visited (singular)
(él/ella)	visit**ó**	he/she visited
(nosotros/as)	visit**amos**	we visited
(vosotros/as)	visit**asteis**	you visited (plural)
(ellos/as)	visit**aron**	they visited

Other **-ar** verbs following this pattern include:

bailar, cantar, comprar, descansar, escuchar, estudiar, hablar, llevar, mandar, montar, pintar, tomar

These verbs have a spelling change in the 'I' form before the **é** ending:

jugar – jug**u**é, navegar – naveg**u**é, sacar – sa**qu**é

The **g** of the infinitive becomes **gu** and the **c** becomes **qu** to keep the sounds (*g* and *k*) the same before the letter **é**. The **u** is silent.

Exercise 10

Write out each sentence using the correct preterite form of the verb given. Then translate the sentences into English.

1 Mis hermanos ~~~~ monumentos. (visitar – *they*)
   – *Mis hermanos visitaron monumentos.*
   My brothers visted monuments.
2 Mi amigo y yo ~~~~ en la discoteca. (bailar – *we*)
3 Carmen ~~~~ en bicicleta. (montar – *she*)
4 ¿~~~~ música? (escuchar – *you, singular*)
5 Fui a la playa y ~~~~. (descansar – *I*)
6 Diego y Juan, ¿~~~~ el sol? (tomar – *you, plural*)
7 Los chicos ~~~~ al fútbol. (jugar – *they*)
8 Fui a la discoteca pero no ~~~~. (bailar – *I*)

	-er **verbs**	
	comer – *to eat*	
(yo)	com**í**	*I ate*
(tú)	com**iste**	*you ate (singular)*
(él/ella)	com**ió**	*he/she ate*
(nosotros/as)	com**imos**	*we ate*
(vosotros/as)	com**isteis**	*you ate (plural)*
(ellos/as)	com**ieron**	*they ate*

	-ir **verbs**	
	salir – *to go out*	
(yo)	sal**í**	*I went out*
(tú)	sal**iste**	*you went out (singular)*
(él/ella)	sal**ió**	*he/she went out*
(nosotros/as)	sal**imos**	*we went out*
(vosotros/as)	sal**isteis**	*you went out (plural)*
(ellos/as)	sal**ieron**	*they went out*

Other **-er** verbs following this pattern include: **beber**

Other **-ir** verbs following this pattern include: **compartir**, **escribir**, **recibir**

Exercise 11

Choose the correct verb form to complete each sentence. Write out the sentences and translate them into English.

1 Por la tarde fui al cafetería y **bebí / bebió** limonada.
2 Carmen y Ana **comiste / comieron** helado.

3 Miguel **recibí / recibió** unos regalos.
4 ¿**Salí / Saliste** con tu amiga?
5 Fuimos a un bar y **bebimos / bebisteis** vino.
6 Antonio **escribí / escribió** una carta.
7 El miércoles no **salí / salisteis**: escuché música en mi dormitorio.
8 Diego y Juan **recibió / recibieron** unos mensajes de su amigo.

(b) *ir/ser*

The verbs **ir** and **ser** are irregular in the preterite. They are also unusual in both having exactly the same forms. The context makes it clear which verb is meant.

	ir – *to go*	
(yo)	fui	*I went*
(tú)	fuiste	*you went (singular)*
(él/ella)	fue	*he/she went*
(nosotros/as)	fuimos	*we went*
(vosotros/as)	fuisteis	*you went (plural)*
(ellos/as)	fueron	*they went*

	ser – *to be*	
(yo)	fui	*I was*
(tú)	fuiste	*you were (singular)*
(él/ella)	fue	*he/she was*
(nosotros/as)	fuimos	*we were*
(vosotros/as)	fuisteis	*you were (plural)*
(ellos/as)	fueron	*they were*

Exercise 12

Translate the sentences into English, using the context to work out whether each verb is from **ir** *(to go)* or **ser** *(to be)*.

1 ¿Fuiste a Madrid en avión?
   – *Did you go to Madrid by plane?*
2 Fue a Alemania con su familia.
3 Fue muy aburrido.
4 El año pasado fuimos a Granada.
5 Fueron de vacaciones en barco.
6 Mi viaje a Argentina fue estupendo.
7 ¿Adónde fuiste?
8 ¿Cómo fue?
9 ¿Fuisteis en coche?
10 Fui a un restaurante. Fue muy caro.

4.5 Recognising different tenses

It's important to recognise which tense is being used in speech or texts, and to use the correct tenses in your own speaking and writing. Look for key time expressions to help you.

+ present tense	+ near future tense	+ preterite
normalmente voy … *normally I go …* **generalmente** juego … *usually I play …* **todos los días** llevo … *every day I wear …* **los fines de semana** escucho … *at weekends I listen to …*	**mañana** voy a ir … *tomorrow I'm going to go …* **pasado mañana** voy a jugar … *the day after tomorrow I'm going to play …* **la próxima vez** voy a llevar … *next time I'm going to wear …* **este fin de semana** voy a ver … *this weekend I'm going to watch …*	**ayer** fui … *yesterday I went …* **anteayer** jugué … *the day before yesterday I played …* **el fin de semana pasado** compré … *last weekend I bought …* **el año pasado** monté … *last year I rode …* **el invierno pasado** descansé … *last winter I rested …* **el verano pasado** visité … *last summer I visited …*

Exercise 13

Rewrite these sentences, using the **near future tense** in place of the present.

1 Normalmente voy al cine. Mañana …
 – *Mañana voy a ir al cine.*
2 Los fines de semana Carmen va a la piscina. Este fin de semana Carmen …
3 Por la tarde Juan escucha música. Esta tarde Juan …
4 Generalmente hago mucho deporte. Mañana …

Now rewrite these sentences, using the **present tense** in place of the future.

5 El jueves voy a hacer esquí. Los jueves …
 – *Los jueves hago esquí.*
6 Mañana Enrique va a hablar por teléfono. Por la mañana Enrique …
7 Más tarde vamos a bailar. Normalmente …
8 ¿Este fin de semana vais a jugar con el ordenador? Los fines de semana …

Exercise 14

Rewrite these sentences, using the **present tense** in place of the preterite.

1 El año pasado fui a Madrid. Normalmente …
 – *Normalmente voy a Madrid.*
2 El viernes pasado Juan fue de compras. Los viernes …

3 El verano pasado descansamos en la playa. Generalmente …
4 El sábado pasado Diego y María bailaron. Los sábados …

Now rewrite these sentences, using the **preterite** in place of the present tense.

5 Los fines de semana mi amiga escucha música. El fin de semana pasado …
 – *El fin de semana pasado escuchó música.*
6 En el verano tomamos el sol. El verano pasado …
7 Normalmente voy a Escocia. El año pasado …
8 Los jueves juegan al fútbol. El jueves pasado …

Exercise 15

Past, present or future? Use each set of prompts to write a sentence using the appropriate tense.

1 yesterday – go shopping – I
 – *Ayer fui de compras.*
2 usually – wear jeans – we
3 last year – go to France – she
4 tomorrow – sunbathe – I
5 next time – see a film – he
6 at weekends – play football – they
7 last summer – buy a T-shirt – I

Gramática

4.6 Making verbs negative

To make a sentence or a question negative, put **no** before the verb.

No voy a ir al cine.
  I'm not going to go to the cinema.
¿Qué **no** te gusta?   *What don't you like?*

You can make a negative opinion with **no** stronger by adding **nada**.

No le gusta **nada** ir de compras.
  *He doesn't like going shopping **at all**.*

nunca (*never*) also goes before the verb.

Nunca es aburrida.   *She is never boring.*

4.7 me gusta, etc.

(a) me gusta/me gustan + noun
me gusta (*I like*) literally means *it is pleasing to me*. If you are talking about liking more than one thing, use **me gustan** (literally: *they are pleasing to me*).

To say *you like*, use **te gusta/te gustan**. To say *he/she likes*, use **le gusta/le gustan**.

	+ singular noun	+ plural noun
I like	**me gusta** la ópera	**me gustan** las películas
you like	**te gusta** el fútbol	**te gustan** los libros
he/she likes	**le gusta** la música	**le gustan** los cómics

The expressions **me encanta** (*I love* – literally: *it delights me*) and **me interesa** (*I'm interested in* – literally: *it interests me*) follow the same patterns.

To make it clear who you are talking about, add **a** + the person's name.

A Carmen le encanta la natación.

You must include the definite article (**el/la/los/las**) with the noun.

Me interesa **la** música.   *I'm interested in music.*

(b) me gusta + verb
me gusta, **me encanta** and **me interesa** can also be followed by another verb in the infinitive. (Note that the plural forms, **me gustan** etc., are not used in this way.)

Me gusta **navegar** por internet.
  I like to surf the net.
A Diego **le encanta jugar** al fútbol.
  Diego loves to play football.

Exercise 16
Write out the sentences, using the correct verb form and pronoun (**me**, **te** or **le**).

1 Voy a un concierto porque ～ (interesar) la música. – *Voy a un concierto porque me interesa la música.*
2 A Javier ～ (encantar) los videojuegos.
3 ～ (gustar) mucho mandar mensajes a mis amigos.
4 ¿ ～ (gustar) el Real Madrid, Diego?
5 María odia el fútbol. ¡No ～ (gustar) nada!
6 A mi hermana no ～ (interesar) bailar.
7 ¿Qué ～ (gustar) hacer, Sergio?
8 Al perro ～ (gustar) las galletas.

4.8 se puede/se pueden

The verb forms **se puede** and **se pueden** (from **poder** – *to be able*, '*can*') mean '*you can*'. They are followed by another verb in the infinitive.

Use **se puede** when referring to one thing and **se pueden** when referring to more than one.

Se puede comprar carne en una carnicería.
  You can buy meat in a butcher's.
Se pueden comprar libros en una librería.
  You can buy books in a bookshop.

Exercise 17
se puede or **se pueden**? For each item in the first box, write a sentence saying where it can be bought, choosing a shop from the second box.

Se puede comprar carne en una carnicería.

~~carne~~ CDs comida joyas libros pan pasteles zapatos	una pastelería un supermercado una zapatería ~~una carnicería~~ una joyería una panadería una tienda de música una librería

4.9 Verbs with the infinitive

Some verbs can be followed by another verb in the infinitive. For example:

me gusta	I like
me encanta	I love
me interesa	I am interested in
odio	I hate
prefiero	I prefer
me gustaría	I would like
puedo*	I can
se puede(n)*	you can
quiero*	I want
tengo que*	I have to
voy a*	I'm going to

* See section **4.2(b)** for all forms of **querer** and **poder** and section **4.2(d)** for all forms of **tener** and **ir** in the present tense.

Me gusta **ver** la televisión.
   I like watching/to watch television.
Me encanta **escuchar** música.
   I love listening/to listen to music.
Odio **ordenar** mi dormitorio.
   I hate tidying my room.
Prefiere **salir** con sus amigos.
   He prefers going out/to go out with friends.
¿Te gustaría **ver** el partido?
   Would you like to watch the match?
Podemos **jugar** a los bolos.
   We can go bowling.
No se pueden **llevar** vaqueros en mi instituto.
   You can't wear jeans at my school.
¿Quieres **ir** al cine?
   Do you want to go to the cinema?
Tiene que **hacer** sus deberes.
   She has to do her homework.
Voy a **salir** con mis amigos.
   I'm going to go out with my friends.

5 Prepositions

A preposition is a word or phrase showing the relationship of one thing to another, e.g. 'on top of', 'behind', 'after'.

a	to
a la derecha de	to the right of
a la izquierda de	to the left of
al final de	at the end of
al lado de	beside
de	from, of
debajo de	under
delante de	in front of
después de	after
detrás de	behind
en	in, at
encima de	on (top of)
entre … y	between … and
para	for

The preposition **de** can also refer to who/what something belongs to.

la habitación **de** mi hermano   *my brother's room*
(literally: *the room of my brother*)

de + el
When **de** (*of*) is followed by **el**, **de + el** merge to make **del**. But **de + la** remain separate.

detrás **del** ordenador	*behind the computer*
delante **de la** casa	*in front of the house*

a + el
When **a** (*to*) is followed by **el**, they merge to make **al**. But **a + la** remain separate.

Fui **al** acuario.	*I went to the aquarium.*
Voy **a la** playa.	*I am going to the beach.*

6 Question words

Spanish question words always have an accent.

¿a qué hora?	at what time?
¿adónde?	(to) where?
¿cómo?	how?, what … like?
¿cuál?	which one?
¿cuáles?	which ones?
¿cuándo?	when?
¿cuánto/cuánta?*	how much?
¿cuántos/cuántas?*	how many?
¿dónde?	where?
¿por qué?	why?
¿qué?	what?
¿quién?	who?

*These words change to agree with a noun.

Vocabulario español–inglés

A

a *to*
a las (ocho) *at (eight) o'clock*
a menudo *often*
¿a qué hora? *at what time?*
abajo *downstairs, below*
la abertura *hole, opening*
el abrigo *coat*
aburrido/a *boring*
¡qué aburrido! *how boring!*
la aceituna *olive*
acostarse *to go to bed*
la actividad *activity*
actual *current, actual*
el acuario *aquarium*
de acuerdo *OK*
estar de acuerdo (con) *to agree (with)*
me acuesto *I go to bed*
además *also, in addition*
adiós *goodbye*
¿adónde? *(to) where?*
el agente secreto *secret agent*
agradable *pleasant*
el agua *water*
ahora *now*
el ajedrez *chess*
al/a la *to the*
las albóndigas *meatballs*
Alemania *Germany*
algo *anything, something*
¿algo más? *anything else?*
algunas veces *a few times*
allí *there*
alto/a *tall*
amarillo/a *yellow*
América del Sur *South America*
la amiga *friend (f)*
el amigo *friend (m)*
la anchoa *anchovy*
andar en monopatín *to skateboard*
andino *Andean (from the Andes)*
el ángel *angel*
animado/a *excited, animated*
el año (pasado) *(last) year*
anteayer *the day before yesterday*
anticuado/a *old-fashioned, out of date*
antiguo/a *old, ancient*
aquí *here*
la araña *spider*
Argentina *Argentina*
argentino/a *Argentinian*
la arquitecta *architect (f)*
el arquitecto *architect (m)*
la arquitectura *architecture*
el arroz (pl. arroces) *rice, rice dish*
las artes circenses *circus arts*
el artista *artist (m)*
la artista *artist (f)*
¡qué asco! *how disgusting!*
así que *so, thus*
atractivo/a *attractive*

el atún *tuna*
aunque *although*
en autocar *by coach*
la aventura *adventure*
en avión *by plane*
ayer *yesterday*
azul *blue*

B

bailar *to dance/go dancing*
bailé *I danced*
el baile de disfraces *fancy dress ball*
bailo *I dance*
bajo/a *short (person)*
las Baleares *the Balearic Islands*
el balneario *spa*
el bañador *swimsuit*
barato/a *cheap*
en barco *by boat*
la barra de pan *baguette, loaf of bread*
el barrio *district*
el barrio gótico *the Gothic quarter (of Barcelona)*
bastante *enough*
beber *to drink*
bebí *I drank*
bebimos *we drank*
bebo *I drink*
bello/a *beautiful*
la berenjena *aubergine*
en bicicleta *by bike*
el bigote *moustache*
el billete *ticket*
blanco/a *white*
el bocadillo *sandwich*
la bolera *bowling alley*
la bolsa *bag*
bonito/a *nice, pretty*
¡qué bonito es! *how beautiful (it is)!*
el bosque tropical *tropical rainforest*
las botas *boots*
la botella de agua *bottle of water*
el botón *button*
la bruja *witch*
¡buen viaje! *have a good trip!*
¡buenas noches! *good night!*
bueno … *well …*
bueno/a *good*

C

el caballero *gentleman*
el caballo *horse*
el cacao *cocoa*
el café *coffee*
la cafetería *café*
calcula *calculate (command)*
la calle *street*
¡qué calor! *it's so hot!*
la cama *bed*
la camisa *shirt*

la camiseta *T-shirt*
la camiseta de fútbol *football shirt*
el campo *countryside*
el canal *canal*
la canción *song*
el cangrejo *crab*
el cantante *singer (m)*
la cantante *singer (f)*
cantar *to sing*
la capa *cape*
Caperucita *Little Red Riding Hood*
la capital *capital*
el caracol *snail*
el carácter *character*
caribeño/a *Caribbean*
la carne *meat*
el carné de identidad *identity card*
la carnicería *butcher's*
caro/a *expensive*
la carta *menu*
el cartón (de leche) *carton (of milk)*
la casa *house*
el casino *casino*
castaño *brown (hair)*
catalán *Catalan (language)*
el catálogo *catalogue*
la cebolla *onion*
cenar *to have dinner/supper*
Cenicienta *Cinderella*
ceno *I have dinner/supper*
el céntimo *cent*
el centro *centre (of the town)*
el centro comercial *the shopping centre*
cerca *near*
los cereales *cereal*
la cerveza *beer*
la cesta *basket*
chatear por internet *to chat online*
el chico *boy*
me chifla(n) *I love, I adore*
chileno/a *Chilean*
el chocolate con churros *hot chocolate with doughnuts*
el chorizo *chorizo (spicy sausage)*
chulo/a *great*
el cibercafé *internet café*
el cielo *sky*
cien *100*
el cine *cinema*
la ciudad *city*
la civilización *civilization*
la clase *type, class*
en coche *by car*
la cocina *kitchen*
el cocodrilo *crocodile*
el cóctel *cocktail*
el Cola Cao *Cola Cao (drinking chocolate)*
el cole *school (slang)*
la colección *collection*
el colegio *school*

colombiano/a   Colombian
Colón   (Christopher) Columbus
el   color   colour
de qué color son sus ojos?   what colour are his/her eyes?
y   colorín colorado este cuento se ha terminado   and they all lived happily ever after
el   comedor   dining room
comer   to eat
comí   I ate
el   cómic   comic
la   comida   food, meal, lunch
comió   he/she ate, he/she had for lunch
comiste   you ate, you had for lunch
como   I eat, I have for lunch
¿cómo?   how?, what … like?
¿cómo es?   what is he/she like?, what does he/she look like?
¿cómo estás?   how are you?
¿cómo fue?   what was it like?
¿cómo fuiste?   how did you go?
¿cómo te llamas?   what's your name?
cómodo/a   comfortable
compartimos   we share/we shared
compartir   to share
comprar   to buy
ir de compras   to go shopping
compraste   you bought
compré   I bought
compró   he/she bought
¡compruébalo!   check it out (command)
con   with
el   concierto   concert
el   concurso   competition
conmigo   with me
conocí a   I got to know
es conocido/a   is known
el   consejo   advice
consiste (en)   it consists (of)
contar   to tell, to count
el   continente   continent
contorneado/a   twisted
convirtió (en)   he/she/it changed/converted (into)
la   corbata   tie
el   correo electrónico   email, email address
corto/a   short
la   cosa   thing
otra cosa   something else
la   costa   coast
la   costumbre   custom, habit
creado/a   created
creo que   I think that
cruza   cross (command)
cruzamos   we cross
de cuadros   checked
¿cuál(es)?   which one(s)?
¿cuál es tu nacionalidad?   what is your nationality?

¿cuál(es) prefieres?   which one(s) do you prefer?
¿cuándo?   when?
¿cuánto cuesta?   how much is it?
¿cuánto tiempo pasaste allí?   how much time did you spend there?
¿cuántos años tienes?   how old are you?
el   cuarto de baño   bathroom
Cuba   Cuba
cubano/a   Cuban
la   cucaracha   cockroach
la   cuenta   bill
el   cuento   story
de   cuero   leather
el   cumpleaños   birthday
la   curva   curve

D

de   of, about
los   deberes   homework
decidir   to decide
decir   to say
la   defensa   defence
del   of the (m)
delante de   in front of
delgado/a   slim
delicioso/a   delicious
demasiado   too (much)
la   democracia   democracy
el   deporte   sport
a la   derecha   to the right
el   desastre   disaster
desayunar   to have breakfast
desayuno   I have breakfast
descansar   to rest
descansé   I rested
desde   from
desovar   to lay eggs
despertarse   to wake up
me   despierto   I wake up
después   afterwards
después de   after …ing
el   destino   destination
detrás de   behind
el   día   day
diario/a   daily
el   dibujo   art
dice   he/she/it says
dicen   they say
dices   you say
la   dictadura   dictatorship
el   diente   tooth
la   dieta   diet
diferente   different
dime   tell me (command)
el   dinero   money
la   dirección   direction
la   discoteca   disco
el   diseñador   designer (m)
la   diseñadora   designer (f)
diseñar   to design
el   diseño   design
el   disfraz   disguise

disfruta   enjoy (command)
disfrutar   to enjoy
divertido/a   amusing, entertaining
dobla   turn (command)
el   dólar   dollar
el   domingo   Sunday
donde   where
¿dónde?   where?
¿dónde está?   where is?
¿dónde quedamos?   where shall we meet?
dorado/a   golden
dormir   to sleep
ducharse   to shower
me   ducho   I shower
duerme   sleep (command)
durante   during

E

la   edad   age
el   edificio   building
el   ejemplo   example
electrónico/a   electronic
elegir   to choose
el   elemento   element
elige   choose (command)
eligió   he/she/it chose
el   emperador   emperor
(no)   empieces   (don't) start (command)
en   in, at, by
en tal caso   in that case
le   encanta(n)   he/she loves
me   encanta(n)   I love
enfrente   opposite
la   ensalada   salad
entonces   then
la   entrada   ticket
el   entrante   starter
entrar   to enter
el   equipo   team
érase una vez …   once upon a time there was …
eres   you (sing.) are
es   he/she is
la   esclava   slave (f)
el   esclavo   slave (m)
escocés/escocesa   Scottish
Escocia   Scotland
escuchar   to listen
escuché   I listened
escucho   I listen
la   escultura   sculpture
esencial   essential
España   Spain
español(a)   Spanish
especial   special
la   especialidad   speciality
la   especie   species
esperar   to hope
espero   I hope
el   esquí (acuático)   (water) skiing
los   esquís   skis
está   he/she/it is
esta(s)   this (these) (f)

el estadio   stadium
estadounidense   North American
Estados Unidos   United States
estáis   you (plural) are
estamos   we are
estampado/a   patterned
están   they are
estar   to be
estás   you (sing.) are
las estatuas vivientes   living statues
este   this (m)
el estilo   style
estos   these (m pl)
estoy   I am
estoy de vacaciones   I'm on holiday
la estrella   star, celebrity
estudiar   to study
estudias   you study
estudió   he/she studied
estupendo/a   fantastic
el examen   exam
la excursión   excursion, trip
el explorador   explorer
explorar   to explore

F

la falda   skirt
famoso/a   famous
fantástico/a   fantastic
la fauna   fauna
favorito/a   favourite
la fe   faith
la fecha de nacimiento   date of birth
feo/a   ugly
la fiesta   party, festival
el fin de semana   weekend
al final   in the end
el flan   crème caramel
la flora   flora
de flores   flowery
la forma   form, shape
el foro   forum (internet)
Francia   France
frecuentemente   frequently
la fresa   strawberry
frito/a   fried
la fruta   fruit
fue   he/she/it was, he/she/it went
fui   I was, I went
fuimos   we were, we went
el fútbol   football
el futbolín   table football

G

las gafas de sol   sunglasses
la galería de arte   art gallery
Gales   Wales
galés/galesa   Welsh
la galleta   biscuit
la gamba   prawn

gana   he/she/it wins
el ganador   winner (m)
la ganadora   winner (f)
ganar   to win
tener ganas   to want to
el gato   cat
el gaucho   cowboy
generalmente   usually
generoso/a   generous
genial   brilliant
el genio   genius
la gente   people
el girasol   sunflower
la gorra   cap
la gótica   goth (f)
el gótico   goth (m)
gracias   thank you
el gramo   gram
grande   big, large
grasiento/a   greasy
Grecia   Greece
griego/a   Greek
gris   grey
el grupo   group
guapo/a   good-looking, attractive
el guardarropa   wardrobe
guay   great, cool
¡qué guay!   how wonderful!
el gusano   worm
le gusta(n)   he/she likes
me gusta(n)   I like
me gustaría   I would like (to)
¿te gustaría …?   would you like (to) …?
el gusto   taste
me gustó   I liked it

H

el hábitat   habitat
habitual   usual
habitualmente   usually
hablador(a)   talkative, chatty
hablar   to talk, to speak
hablo   I talk, I speak
hace buen tiempo   it's good/ nice weather
hace viento   it's windy
hacer   to do, to make
hacer mis deberes   to do my homework
haces   you do, you make
hago   I do, I make
la hamburguesa   hamburger
hasta   as far as, until
hasta luego   see you later
hasta pronto   see you soon
hay   there is/there are
hecho/a (de)   made (of)
el helado (de chocolate)   (chocolate) ice-cream
herbívoro/a   herbivorous
la hermana   sister
el hermano   brother
hermoso/a   wonderful, beautiful

hice   I did
histórico/a   historic
hizo   he/she/it did, he/she/it made
¡hola!   hello!
el hombre   man
horrible   awful
hoy   today
húmedo/a   humid

I

la idea   idea
el ídolo   idol
la iglesia   church
la imagen   image
el imperio   empire
importante   important
imposible   impossible
impresionante   impressive
incómodo/a   uncomfortable
independiente   independent
industrial   industrial
la influencia   influence
la informática   ICT, computing
Inglaterra   England
inglés/inglesa   English
el inicio   start, home (internet)
inolvidable   unforgettable
el insecto   insect
el instituto   college
inteligente   intelligent
intenta   he/she/it tries
me interesa(n)   I'm interested in
internacional   international
íntimo/a   intimate
el invierno   winter
ir   to go
Irlanda   Ireland
irlandés/irlandesa   Irish
la isla   island
Italia   Italy
italiano/a   Italian
a la izquierda   to the left

J

el jaguar   jaguar (animal)
el jamón (serrano)   (cured) ham
el jersey   jumper
joven   young
las joyas   jewellery
la joyería   jeweller's
juego   I play
el juego   game
el jueves   Thursday
el jugador   player (m)
la jugadora   player (f)
jugar a los bolos   to go bowling
jugar al fútbol   to play football
jugar al futbolín   to play table football
jugué   I played
juntos/as   together

L

la laguna   *lagoon*
la lana   *wool*
largo/a   *long*
me lavo el pelo   *I wash my hair*
me lavo los dientes   *I brush my teeth*
la leche   *milk*
la lechuga   *a lettuce*
levantarse   *to get up*
me levanto   *I get up*
la librería   *bookshop*
el libro   *book*
la limonada   *lemonade*
el litro   *litre*
llamarse   *to be called*
se llama   *his/her name is*
llamado/a   *called*
me llamo   *my name is*
la llanura   *plain (land)*
llevar   *to wear*
llevé   *I wore*
llevo   *I wear*
llevó   *he/she wore*
el lolailo   *fan of cheesy music*
el lomo   *loin of pork*
luego   *then*
el lujo   *luxury*
de lunares   *spotted*
el lunes   *Monday*

M

la madre   *mother*
la magdalena   *fairy cake*
mágico/a   *magic*
el maíz   *maize, corn*
mal   *bad/badly*
mañana   *tomorrow*
el manatí   *manatee (animal)*
mandar   *to send*
mandé   *I sent*
mando   *I send*
de manga corta   *short-sleeved*
de manga larga   *long-sleeved*
sin mangas   *sleeveless*
la manzana   *apple*
el mar (Caribe)   *(Caribbean) sea*
la marca   *brand*
los mariscos   *seafood*
marrón   *brown*
el martes   *Tuesday*
más   *more, most*
más … que   *more … than*
medio/a   *half*
medio kilo de   *half a kilo of*
mediodía   *midday*
mejor   *better, best*
menos   *less, least*
menos de   *less than*
menos … que   *less … than*
el mensaje   *message, text*
el mercado   *market*
merendar   *to have tea*
meriendo   *for tea I eat*
el mes   *month*

mexicano/a   *Mexican*
México   *Mexico*
mí   *me*
mi(s)   *my*
mide   *he/she/it is … tall*
¡qué miedo!   *how frightening!*
el miércoles   *Wednesday*
mil   *thousand*
mirar   *to look at*
mirar escaparates   *to go window-shopping*
de moda   *in fashion*
modernista   *modernist*
la momia   *mummy*
el mono   *monkey*
en monopatín   *by skateboard*
la montaña   *mountain*
la montaña rusa   *rollercoaster*
montar a caballo   *to go horse riding*
montar en bicicleta   *to ride a bike*
montar en las atracciones del parque   *to go on the rides at the funfair*
monté en bicicleta   *I rode my bike*
un montón de cosas   *a heap of things*
el monumento   *monument, sight*
moreno   *dark (hair)*
el mosaico de cerámica   *mosaic tiles*
la mosca   *fly*
el motivo   *motive, reason*
mucho gusto   *pleased to meet you*
mucho/a   *a lot*
la muerte   *death*
la mujer   *woman*
el mundo   *world*
la muñequera   *wristband*
murió   *he/she died*
el museo   *museum*
la música   *music*
musulmán   *Muslim*
muy   *very*

N

nació   *he/she was born*
la nacionalidad   *nationality*
nada   *nothing*
naranja   *orange*
la natación   *swimming*
los nativos amerindios   *native Americans*
la naturaleza   *nature*
navegar por   *to navigate*
necesitas   *you need*
negro/a   *black*
¡ni en sueños!   *in your dreams!*
¡ni hablar!   *no way!*
la niña   *child (girl)*
no   *not*
¡no es justo!   *it's not fair!*

no importa   *it doesn't matter*
no me gusta (nada)   *I don't like (at all)*
no me gustó   *I didn't like*
no pasa nada   *it doesn't matter*
¡no sé por qué!   *I don't know why*
no seas negativo/a   *don't be negative (command)*
la noche   *night*
el nombre   *name*
el noreste   *northeast*
normal   *normal*
normalmente   *normally*
el norte   *north*
la novia   *girlfriend*
el novio   *boyfriend*
nuestro/a   *our*
nuevo/a   *new*
el número   *number*
nunca   *never*

O

o   *or*
la obra   *work*
obtener   *to obtain*
el Occidente   *the West*
odio   *I hate*
ondulado/a   *wavy*
la opción   *option*
la ópera   *opera*
la opinión   *opinion*
el ordenador   *computer*
ordenar (mi dormitorio)   *to tidy (my room)*
oriental   *oriental, eastern*
el origen   *origin*

P

el padre   *father*
los padres   *parents*
la paella (de mariscos)   *(seafood) paella*
el pájaro   *bird*
el pan   *bread*
la panadería   *baker's, bread shop*
los pantalones   *trousers*
las papas   *potatoes*
para   *for, in order to*
el parque   *park*
el parque de atracciones   *amusement park, funfair*
el partido   *game, match*
pasado mañana   *the day after tomorrow*
pasando   *passing*
pasar   *to spend*
el pasatiempo   *hobby, pastime*
pasé   *I spent*
¡lo pasé bien!   *I had a good time!*
¡lo pasé bomba!   *I had a fantastic time!*

¡lo pasé fenomenal! *I had a wonderful time!*
¡lo pasé guay! *I had a great time!*
¡lo pasé mal! *I had a bad time!*
pasear al perro *to walk the dog*
el paseo *walk*
la pasta *pasta*
el pastel *cake*
la pastelería *cake shop*
la patata *potato*
las patatas bravas *spicy potatoes*
las patatas fritas *chips, crisps*
peinarse *to comb/brush one's hair*
me peino *I comb/brush my hair*
la peli *film (slang)*
la película *film*
pelirrojo/a *red (hair)*
la peluquería *hairdresser's*
el peluquero *hairdresser*
pensar *to think*
el pepino *cucumber*
pequeño/a *small*
la pera *pear*
perder *to miss, to lose*
perdido/a *lost*
la perdiz estofada *stewed partridge*
perdón *excuse me*
perezoso/a *lazy*
perfecto/a *perfect*
pero *but*
la persona *person*
el pescado *fish*
el pescador *fisherman*
la pescadora *fisherwoman*
el pez *fish*
pica *he/she pecks*
el pico *pick*
a pie *on foot*
la piedra *stone*
el pijo *posh (m)*
el pimiento *sweet pepper*
pintar *to paint*
pinté *I painted*
la pintura *painting*
la pizza *pizza*
el placer *pleasure*
la plata *money*
el plátano *banana*
el plato *dish*
la playa *beach*
la plaza *square*
un poco *a little*
podéis *you (plural) can*
podemos *we can*
poder *to be able to, can*
el pollo *chicken*
el poncho *poncho*
por *for*
por favor *please*
por la mañana *in the morning*
por la tarde *in the evening*
¿por qué? *why?*
por supuesto *of course*
por último *finally*
porque *because*

Portugal *Portugal*
el postre *dessert*
practicar *to practise*
práctico/a *practical*
precioso/a *wonderful, beautiful*
preferido/a *favourite*
preferir *to prefer*
prefieres *you prefer*
prefiero *I prefer*
el premio *prize*
el presentador *presenter (m)*
la presentadora *presenter (f)*
presentar *to introduce*
el primer plato *starter*
primero *first*
principal *main*
probar *to try*
probé *I tried*
el problema *problem*
proclamado/a *declared*
el profesor *teacher (m)*
la profesora *teacher (f)*
propio/a *own (adj)*
proteger *to protect*
la próxima vez *next time*
el pueblo *village*
puede *he/she can*
pueden *they can*
puedes *you (sing.) can*
puedo *I can*
pues *well*
el pulpo *octopus*
el punto *point*

Q

que *that*
¿qué? *what?*
¿qué haces en tu tiempo libre? *what do you do in your free time?*
¿qué hay? *what is there?*
¿qué hiciste? *what did you do?*
¿qué quieres? *what would you like?*
¿qué tal? *how are you?*
¿qué tal lo pasaste? *what sort of a time did you have?*
me queda *it suits me*
me quedé *I stayed*
me quedo (en casa) *I stay (at home)*
queréis *you (plural) want*
queremos *we want*
querer *to want*
el queso *cheese*
¿quién? *who?, whom?*
quiere *he/she wants*
quieren *they want*
quieres *you (sing.) want*
quiero *I want, I'd like*
te quiero *I love you*
quizás *perhaps*

R

el rabo *tail*
el rabo de toro *bull's tail*
la ración *portion*
la rana *frog*
rápido/a *quick*
los rápidos *rapids*
rarísimo/a *very strange*
el rascacielo *skyscraper*
un rato *a while*
el ratón *mouse*
de rayas *striped*
recibió *he received*
recibir *to receive*
recomendamos *we recommend*
el regalo *a present*
la región *region*
regresar *to return*
regresó *he/she returned*
la reina *queen*
el reinado *reign*
relajarse *to relax*
República Dominicana *the Dominican Republic*
la reserva natural *nature reserve*
responsable *responsible*
restableció *he/she re-established*
el restaurante *restaurant*
el resultado *result*
al revés *backwards*
el rey *king*
¡qué rica! *how delicious!*
rico/a *delicious, tasty*
el ritmo *rhythm*
rizado/a *curly*
robado/a *robbed*
rojo/a *red*
romano/a *Roman*
la ropa *clothes*
rosa *pink*
rubio/a *fair, blond*
la ruta *route*
la rutina diaria *daily routine*

S

el sábado *Saturday*
sacar fotos *to take photos*
sales *you go out*
salgo *I go out*
salí *I went out*
salimos *we went out*
salió *he/she went out*
salir *to go out*
saliste *you went out*
el salón *lounge*
el salón recreativo *the amusement arcade*
las sandalias *sandals*
sano/a *healthy*
el santuario *sanctuary*
saqué fotos *I took photos*

la sauna   *sauna*
el segundo plato   *main course*
la semana   *week*
   señor   *sir*
el señor del universo   *master of the universe*
   señora   *madam*
   ser   *to be*
   serio/a   *serious*
la serpiente   *snake*
   servido/a   *served*
   severo/a   *strict*
   si   *if*
   siempre   *always*
lo siento   *I'm sorry*
   sigue todo recto   *go straight on*
   siguiente   *following, next*
   simpático/a   *nice*
   sin duda   *without doubt*
   sirven   *they serve*
   sobre todo   *above all*
   sois   *you (plural) are*
   sólo   *only*
el sombrero   *hat*
   somos   *we are*
   son   *they are*
   soñé   *I dreamt*
la sopa   *soup*
   soy   *I am*
   su(s)   *his/her/your (polite)*
la sudadera   *sweatshirt*
el sueño   *dream*
la sugerencia   *suggestion*
el supermercado   *supermarket*
el superviviente   *survivor*
el sur   *south*
   surrealista   *surrealist*

T

de tacón   *high-heeled*
   también   *also*
   tampoco   *neither*
   tanto en común   *so much in common*
   tanto tiempo   *so much time*
el tapeo   *eating tapas*
   tarde   *late*
el té   *tea*
el teatro   *theatre*
la televisión   *television*
la tendencia   *trend*
   tenéis   *you (plural) have*
   tenemos   *we have*
   tenemos miedo   *we are frightened*
   tener   *to have*
   tener mucho en común   *to have a lot in common*
   tener que   *to have to*
   tengo   *I have*
   tengo catorce años   *I am 14*
   tengo hambre   *I'm hungry*
   tengo que   *I have to*
   tengo sed   *I'm thirsty*
   tengo suerte   *I'm lucky*

no tengo tiempo   *I don't have any time*
la terraza   *terrace*
el tiburón   *shark*
el tiempo libre   *free time*
la tienda   *tent, shop*
la tienda de música   *music shop*
la tienda de ropa   *clothes shop*
   tiene   *he/she has*
   tienen   *they have*
   tienes   *you (sing.) have*
el tigre   *tiger*
   típico/a   *typical*
el tipo   *type*
   todo/a   *all*
de todas maneras   *anyway*
   todo el tiempo   *all the time*
   todos los días   *every day*
   toma   *take (command)*
   tomar   *to take*
   tomar el sol   *to sunbathe*
el tomate   *tomato*
   tomé el sol   *I sunbathed*
la torre   *tower*
la tortilla   *omelette*
la tortuga   *tortoise*
la(s) tostada(s)   *toast*
   totalmente   *totally*
   trabajar   *to work*
el traje   *suit*
la tranquilidad   *peace*
   tranquilo/a   *quiet*
el trasto   *bowl*
   trata de   *it's about*
el tren (minero)   *(mining) train*
en tren   *by train*
las tribus urbanas   *urban tribes*
el trigo   *wheat*
   triste   *sad*
el trozo   *slice*
   tu(s)   *your*
el turista   *tourist (m)*
la turista   *tourist (f)*
   turística   *tourist (adj)*
   tuve que   *I had to*

U

   último/a   *last*
el uniforme (escolar)   *(school) uniform*
   usted   *you (polite)*
   utilizar   *to use*
   utilizó   *he/she/it used*
las uvas   *grapes*

V

va   *he/she/it goes*
las vacaciones   *holidays*
   vais   *you go*
   vale   *OK*
   valen   *they cost, they are worth*
   vamos   *we go*
   van   *they go*
los vaqueros   *jeans*

   variado/a   *varied*
la variedad   *variety*
   vas   *you go*
a veces   *sometimes*
la velocidad   *speed*
   venenoso/a   *poisonous*
   venir   *to come*
   veo   *I watch*
   ver   *to watch, to see*
a ver   *let's see*
el verano (pasado)   *(last) summer*
   ¿verdad?   *really?*
   verde   *green*
las verduras   *vegetables*
el vestido   *dress*
la vestimenta (habitual)   *(usual) clothing*
   vestirse   *to get dressed*
una vez   *once*
de vez en cuando   *from time to time*
el viaje   *journey*
la vida   *life*
el vídeo   *video*
el videojuego   *video game*
   viejo/a   *old*
   viene   *he/she/it comes*
el viernes   *Friday*
la Villa Olímpica   *the Olympic Village*
   vino   *he/she/it came*
el vino   *wine*
   violeta   *purple*
   visitamos   *we visited*
   visitar   *to visit*
   visitaste   *you visited*
   visité   *I visited*
   visitó   *he/she visited*
me visto   *I get dressed*
   vivir   *to live*
   vivo   *I live*
   volar   *to fly*
el voleibol   *volleyball*
   vomito   *I vomit*
   vomitó   *he/she vomited*
   voy   *I go*
   voy a (bailar)   *I'm going to (dance)*

Y

y   *and*
yo   *I*
   yo mismo   *I myself*
   yo te quiero   *I love you*

Z

la zanahoria   *carrot*
la zapatería   *shoe shop*
las zapatillas de deporte   *trainers*
los zapatos   *shoes*
el zumo de naranja   *orange juice*

A

about *de, sobre*
afterwards *después*
age *la edad*
to agree (with) *estar de acuerdo (con)*
all the time *todo el tiempo*
also *también*
always *siempre*
I am *soy, estoy*
amusement arcade *el salón recreativo*
amusing *divertido/a*
and *y, e*
anything *algo*
anything else? *¿algo más?*
apple *la manzana*
they are *son, están*
we are *somos, estamos*
you are *eres, estás*
you (pl) are *sois, estáis*
Argentina *Argentina*
Argentinian *argentino/a*
at *en, a*
I ate *comí*
attractive *guapo/a*
awful *horrible*

B

bad *mal*
baguette *la barra de pan*
baker's *la panadería*
beach *la playa*
because *porque*
behind *detrás de*
best *el/la mejor*
better *mejor*
bike *la bicicleta*
bill *la cuenta*
birthday *el cumpleaños*
biscuit *la galleta*
black *negro/a*
blond *rubio/a*
blue *azul*
boat *el barco*
book *el libro*
bookshop *la librería*
boots *las botas*
boring *aburrido/a*
bottle (of water) *la botella (de agua)*
bowling alley *la bolera*
bread *el pan*
brilliant *genial*
brother *el hermano*
brown *castaño (hair), marrón*
to brush my hair *peinarme*
to brush my teeth *lavarme los dientes*
bus *el autobús*
but *pero*
butcher's *la carnicería*
to buy *comprar*
by *en*

C

café *la cafetería*
cake *el pastel*
cake shop *la pastelería*
cap *la gorra*
car *el coche*
carrot *la zanahoria*
carton of milk *el cartón de leche*
cereal *los cereales*
to chat online *chatear por internet*
cheap *barato/a*
checked *de cuadros*
cheese *el queso*
chicken *el pollo*
Chilean *chileno/a*
chips *las patatas fritas*
cinema *el cine*
city *la ciudad*
clothes *la ropa*
clothes shop *la tienda de ropa*
coach *el autocar*
coffee *el café*
Colombian *colombiano/a*
colour *el color*
to comb my hair *peinarme*
comfortable *cómodo/a*
comic *el cómic*
cool *guay*
to cross *cruzar*
Cuba *Cuba*
curly *rizado/a*

D

to dance *bailar*
day *el día*
the day after tomorrow *pasado mañana*
the day before yesterday *anteayer*
dessert *el postre*
direction *la dirección*
disaster *el desastre*
disco *la discoteca*
to do my homework *hacer mis deberes*
to do sport *hacer deporte*
dress *el vestido*
to drink *beber*

E

to eat *comer*
email (address) *el correo electrónico*
England *Inglaterra*
English *inglés/inglesa*
evening *la tarde*
in the evening *por la tarde*
excuse me *perdón*
expensive *caro/a*
eyes *los ojos*

F

family *la familia*
fancy dress ball *el baile de disfraces*
fantastic *estupendo/a, bomba*
father *el padre*
film *la película*
finally *por último*
fine *muy bien*
first *primero*
fish *el pescado*
food *la comida*
on foot *a pie*
football *el fútbol*
football match *el partido de fútbol*
football shirt *la camiseta de fútbol*
for *por, para*
France *Francia*
free time *el tiempo libre*
Friday *el viernes*
friend *el amigo/la amiga*
in front of *delante de*
fruit *la fruta*

G

generous *generoso/a*
Germany *Alemania*
to get dressed *vestirse*
I get up *me levanto*
I go *voy*
to go *ir*
you go *vas*
to go bowling *jugar a los bolos*
to go on the rides at the funfair *montar en las atracciones del parque*
to go out *salir*
to go shopping *ir de compras*
go straight on *sigue todo recto*
I go to bed *me acuesto*
good *buen/bueno/buena*
good night *buenas noches*
have a good trip! *¡buen viaje!*
goodbye *adiós*
grapes *las uvas*
great *guay*
Greece *Grecia*
green *verde*
grey *gris*

H

hair *el pelo*
hairdresser's *la peluquería*
half *medio/a*
ham *el jamón*
hamburger *la hamburguesa*
he/she has *tiene*
to hate *odiar*
I have *tengo*
to have *tener*

to have breakfast *desayunar*
to have dinner/supper *cenar*
to have lunch *comer*
to have tea *merendar*
I have to *tengo que*
to have to *tener que*
helmet *el casco*
her *su(s)*
here *aquí*
high-heeled *de tacón*
his *su(s)*
holidays *las vacaciones*
homework *los deberes*
house *la casa*
how? *¿cómo?*
how are you? *¿qué tal?*
how much? *¿cuánto?*
I'm hungry *tengo hambre*

I

ice-cream *el helado*
in *en*
intelligent *inteligente*
I'm interested in *me interesa(n)*
to introduce *presentar*
Ireland *Irlanda*
Irish *irlandés/irlandesa*
he/she/it is *es, está*
Italy *Italia*

J

jeans *los vaqueros*
jeweller's *la joyería*
jewellery *las joyas*
jumper *el jersey*

K

a kilo of *un kilo de*

L

last (year) *(el año) pasado*
later *más tarde*
lazy *perezoso/a*
leather *de cuero*
left *la izquierda*
lemonade *la limonada*
less *menos*
less ... than *menos ... que*
let's see *a ver*
lettuce *la lechuga*
I like *me gusta(n)*
he/she likes *le gusta(n)*
to listen (to) *escuchar*
long *largo/a*
long-sleeved *de manga larga*
a lot of *mucho/a*
I love *me encanta(n)*
he/she loves *le encanta(n)*

M

main course *el segundo plato*
market *el mercado*
meal *la comida*
meat *la carne*
message *el mensaje*
Mexican *mexicano/a*
Mexico *México*
Monday *el lunes*
month *el mes*
more *más*
more ... than *más ... que*
morning *la mañana*
in the morning *por la mañana*
mother *la madre*
music *la música*
music shop *la tienda de música*
my *mi(s)*

N

my name is *me llamo*
never *nunca*
next time *la próxima vez*
nice *bonito/a*
normally *normalmente*
North American *estadounidense*
not *no*
nothing *nada*
number *el número*

O

at (3) o'clock *a las (tres)*
of *de*
often *a menudo*
OK *de acuerdo, vale*
old *viejo/a*
old-fashioned *anticuado/a*
or *o*
orange *naranja*
orange juice *el zumo de naranja*

P

to paint *pintar*
parents *los padres*
park *el parque*
pasta *la pasta*
patterned *estampado/a*
pear *la pera*
people *la gente*
pink *rosa*
plane *el avión*
to play *jugar*
to play football *jugar al fútbol*
to play table football *jugar al futbolín*
please *por favor*
Portugal *Portugal*

prawns *las gambas*
present *el regalo*
pretty *bonito/a*
problem *el problema*

R

red *pelirrojo (hair), rojo/a*
restaurant *el restaurante*
right (correct) *correcto/a*
right (side) *la derecha*

S

salad *la ensalada*
sandwich *el bocadillo*
Saturday *el sábado*
school *el colegio, el instituto*
Scotland *Escocia*
Scottish *escocés/escocesa*
seafood *los mariscos*
see you later *hasta luego*
see you soon *hasta pronto*
to send *mandar*
serious *serio/a*
shirt *la camisa*
shoe shop *la zapatería*
shoes *los zapatos*
shopping centre *el centro comercial*
short *bajo/a (person), corto/a*
short-sleeved *de manga corta*
I shower *me ducho*
sister *la hermana*
skateboard *el monopatín*
skirt *la falda*
sleeveless *sin mangas*
slim *delgado/a*
something *algo*
sometimes *a veces*
I'm sorry *lo siento*
soup *la sopa*
Spain *España*
Spanish *español(a)*
sports clothes *la ropa de deporte*
spotted *de lunares*
square *la plaza*
stadium *el estadio*
starter *el primer plato*
to stay at home *quedarse en casa*
street *la calle*
striped *de rayas*
summer *el verano*
to sunbathe *tomar el sol*
Sunday *el domingo*
sunglasses *las gafas de sol*
supermarket *el supermercado*
sweatshirt *la sudadera*
swimming *la natación*
swimsuit *el bañador*

Vocabulario inglés—español

T

to take   *tomar*
to take photos   *sacar fotos*
talkative   *hablador(a)*
tall   *alto/a*
tea   *el té*
television   *la televisión*
then   *luego*
there is/are   *hay*
these   *estos/as*
to think   *pensar*
this   *este/a*
Thursday   *el jueves*
to tidy my room   *ordenar mi dormitorio*
tie   *la corbata*
time   *el tiempo*
from time to time   *de vez en cuando*
to   *a*
toast   *la(s) tostada(s)*
today   *hoy*
tomato   *el tomate*
tomorrow   *mañana*
tonight   *esta noche*
tourist   *el turista/la turista*
train   *el tren*
trousers   *los pantalones*
T-shirt   *la camiseta*
Tuesday   *el martes*
to turn   *doblar*

U

ugly   *feo/a*
uncomfortable   *incómodo/a*
uniform   *el uniforme*
to use   *utilizar*
usually   *generalmente*

V

vegetables   *las verduras*
very   *muy*
video game   *el videojuego*
to visit   *visitar*

W

I wake up   *me despierto*
Wales   *Gales*
to walk the dog   *pasear al perro*
I want   *quiero*
to want   *querer*
I was   *fui*
it was   *fue*
to wash my hair   *lavarme el pelo*
to watch   *ver*
water   *el agua*
wavy   *ondulado/a*
to wear   *llevar*
Wednesday   *el miércoles*
week   *la semana*
weekend   *el fin de semana*

well   *bueno, pues, bien*
Welsh   *galés/galesa*
I went   *fui*
we went   *fuimos*
what?   *¿qué?*
what sort of a time did you have?   *¿qué tal lo pasaste?*
what time?   *¿qué hora?*
what was it like?   *¿cómo fue?*
when?   *¿cuándo?*
where?   *¿dónde?*
where (to)?   *¿adónde?*
white   *blanco/a*
who?   *¿quién?*
why?   *¿por qué?*
winter   *el invierno*
with   *con*
wonderful   *fenomenal*
I would like   *me gustaría*
would you like?   *¿te gustaría?*

Y

year   *el año*
yellow   *amarillo/a*
yesterday   *ayer*
young   *joven*
your   *tu(s)*